P9-CBU-844

SKIP

A Framework to Connect
Industrious People with Elderly Land Owners;
Skills to Inherit Property

Paul Wheaton and Mike Haasl

The information in this book is condensed from a larger body of work. As a result, this book conveys ideas, but is not a complete "how to" guide and should not be taken as such. For full details on implementing these ideas, please do your own research. For anything you choose to do as a result of reading this book, the complete list of things that anybody involved in creating this book is obligated to do is:

      possibly point and laugh

© 2022 Paul Wheaton & Mike Haasl

All rights reserved. No portion of this book may be reproduced in any form or by any electronic or mechanical means, including information storage and retrieval systems, without written permission from the authors, except as permitted by U.S. copyright law. For permissions contact skip@permies.com

First printing, 2022.

Cover design, illustrations, and formatting by Bernal Brothers Studio

permies.com/bernal

For errata, suggestions for a second edition, reviews, and comments: permies.com/skip-book

permies.com   richsoil.com

Publisher's Cataloging-in-Publication Data

Names: Wheaton, Paul, author. | Haasl, Mike, author.
Title: SKIP - A Framework to Connect Industrious People with Elderly Land Owners; Skills to Inherit Property / Paul Wheaton ; Mike Haasl.
Identifiers: ISBN 9781737768005 (pbk.) | 9781737768012 (EPUB) |
Subjects: LCSH Sustainable living. | Self-reliant living. | Urban homesteading. | Permaculture. | Sustainable agriculture. | Home economics. | Environmental protection—Citizen participation. |Retirement--Early retirement. BISAC HOUSE & HOME / Sustainable Living | REFERENCE / Personal & Practical Guides | Crafts & Hobbies / Folkcrafts
Classification: LCC S501.2 .W43 2022 | DDC 640 WHE

Other works by Paul Wheaton

- **Building a Better World in Your Backyard - instead of being angry at bad guys** (book)
  permies.com/bwb
- **World Domination Gardening** (3-movie set)
  richsoil.com/wdg
- **Building a Cob Style Rocket Mass Heater** (movie)
  richsoil.com/heat
- **Better Wood Heat: DIY Rocket Mass Heaters** (8-movie set)
  richsoil.com/heat
- **Permaculture Playing Cards**
  richsoil.com/cards
- **Permaculture Design Course** (100-hour recording)
  pdcvid.com
- **Appropriate Technology Course** (77-hour recording)
  pdcvid.com
- **Devious Experiments for a Truly Passive Greenhouse** (movie)
  permies.com/greenhouse
- **Rocket Ovens: More Than a Wood-Fired Pizza Oven** (movie)
  permies.com/oven
- **Full Tour of Wheaton Labs** (movie)
  permies.com/tour
- **Homesteading and Permaculture Podcasts** (over 500)
  permies.com/podcasts
- **Events and permaculture bootcamp**
  wheaton-labs.com
- permies.com
- richsoil.com
- youtube.com/paulwheaton

to Donna Lee Skovlin

for the courage and patience in providing
a wholesome home to a bizarre teenager

~ Paul

to Cara

for enabling a productive journey down the permaculture path

~ Mike

Table of Contents

Part Zero: Introduction

Part One: PEP Badges

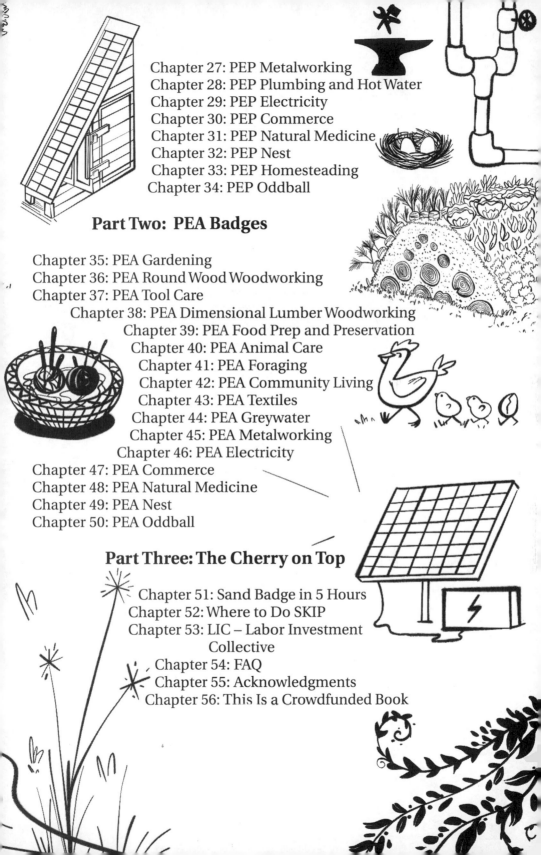

This book is written for:

- industrious people who wish to inherit a homestead
- elderly people with a homestead who desire to find an industrious person who would be a great steward for their property
- people who already have a homestead but wish to build their skills
- people who love permaculture and want to build some hands on experiences
- people who have certain skills and wish to have those skills publicly verified
- people seeking opportunity, rather than land
- parents who wish for their children to gain this sort of substantial experience
- people who feel their life lacks a certain kind of substance, and perhaps, the things they seek are in this very book
- people seeking interns who will arrive with some of these skills
- people applying for competitive internships wanting to improve their chances of being selected
- homestead owners looking for a caretaker or hired help
- people looking for paid positions on homesteads
- people in high school or college who would like to cultivate experiences and skill sets not accessible in the classroom
- people who want to prove that they are industrious
- high school students who wish to have something like a college degree, for free, before they finish their senior year
- homesteaders open to a work trade with an industrious person needing a place to park their tiny home
- people with a tiny home, who need a place to park it, and want to prove that they are industrious
- people who think doing this stuff might make you kinda buff
- people who want to skip the rat race and jump straight to retirement

"If the women don't find you handsome,
they should at least find you handy"

-Red Green

2

The contents of this book started off as a bizarre idea of one giant doofus in overalls. As it grew and started to turn into something substantial, other people jumped in and fleshed out big chunks. Collaborations formed. Hundreds of meetings happened with lots of people. It clearly turned into a big group thing. And somehow it continued to remain presented in first person – as if it was all created by just the doofus.

To make matters worse, we are all certain that this is just the beginning. At every moment, we see that a majority of all this stuff needs a massive overhaul. Again. But the more we overhaul it, the more we want to overhaul it again. And in one of our meetings we came to the conclusion that if we hold off on a book until we are all comfortable with the final product, there will never be a book. So we opted for "take a picture of where we are now" and embrace the idea that we will take a new picture sometime in the future.

It turns out that creating a curriculum is a lot of work. It takes 20 times longer to write a page of a curriculum than to write a page for a normal book. But we feel so strongly about the value of this curriculum that we put in the time.

We are excited about this! A completely free education system. A framework for building useful skills. We can now clearly separate the twenty people who say they accomplish things from the 1 who actually does. Authentic productivity and decency is rewarded.

In all of our meetings, we cannot help but jabber amongst ourselves about how this silly little framework might be the key to solving global problems, while simultaneously rewarding the people who do the work! Will this idea reach millions of people? In time, will there be five times more SKIP classes than Permaculture classes?

Wheeeeeeeeeeeee! Let's go!

permies. com/skip

Chapter 1
My Friend Mike Oehler

You sir, are a kook!

About fifty years ago, my friend Mike Oehler (author of several books including <u>The $50 and Up Underground House Book</u>) bought 45 acres in the panhandle of Idaho just a few hours away from me. During his time on the property, he lent a helping hand to a woman with a property adjacent to his. When she died, she left her 7 acres, house, cars and everything to Mike.

Mike and I talked about every other month. And nearly every time he asked me if I knew of somebody who he could hire to work on his projects. Even more – if they turned out to be good, he wanted to leave his land to them. With every call, his standards for such a person got lower.

Thanks! Backatcha

Mike's property had about eight of his design structures on it – including his latest effort "The Ridgetop House."

Mike's book business was doing quite well and he had two more books ready to publish.

THE $50 & UP UNDERGROUND HOUSE BOOK

The Earth-Sheltered Solar Greenhouse Book

Mike Oehler's

LOW-COST UNDERGROUND HOUSE WORKSHOPS & SURVIVAL SHELTER SEMINARS

4

Mike wanted to will everything, including the book business, the house and cars he inherited, his bank account (pretty healthy)… everything… to one industrious person. He wanted them to come out and prove their industriousness for a few months. Over the decades, there have been about 100 people who came to Mike's place with the idea of building something rather permanent – to be a long time or permanent part of Mike's empire. They are all gone. Mike told me a lot of the stories. True comedy. Some ended up leaving because they were frustrated with Mike being… well… Mike. And some left because Mike ran 'em off.

In one conversation, Mike thought I would have an answer for him if he said the same thing in a louder and angrier voice. Maybe that worked. I did share Mike's message with a lot of potential folks. One fella from my place went up to Mike's and stayed about two months before Mike died. Groundhog day 2016 – especially fitting for a dude who was so into digging.

Everything went to Mike's niece. Who sold it off. The end.

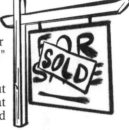

I have heard from dozens of people offering land like this. When I share the stories, I hear from lots of folks who say "I'll take the land!" but I am not aware of their accomplishments.

Mike's stories were heavy with people talking about their accomplishments, only for Mike to discover that nearly all of it was fiction. This wasted Mike's time and energy.

In the meantime, thousands of honest, decent and industrious people went off and got industrious jobs, read Mike's book and pined for the day that they could escape the rat race, buy land someplace like Idaho and start to build something according to Mike's designs. The thought never occurred to them that there could be a shortcut.

Mike was willing to change his will the moment I gave him the name of just one person who I knew for certain had actually accomplished something substantial. I told him about my idea for SKIP and he felt that would be even better.

STUDENT LOANS

COLLEGE

Dozens of times per year I am asked: "I want to live a permaculture life, so which university offers a four-year permaculture degree?"

There are some that do. Of course, they are part of an ag (agricultural) college which is most likely in bed with a chem-ag organization. I've heard some good things about some programs, but I can't help but think that the good people making those programs have to swim upstream to keep them that way. Plus, universities incubate the very worst office politics.

I did the college thing many decades ago. Since my time, the cost has risen by a factor of ten and the quality, I am told, has dropped dramatically. When most people are done with college, they are left with a massive debt. In addition, they struggle to get work that pays enough to make a dent in that debt.

Price

Quality

Time

If you get a 4-year university degree in permaculture, did you build a pond? A shed? A rocket mass heater? Was there a class in hugelkultur? What grade did you get for growing 4 million calories of food? Or was everything you did on paper?

I think there are a lot of good things to say about going to college. There are the experiences inside and outside of the classroom. The lifelong friends. Foundations in writing, math and history. And, most importantly, developing the skills to navigate through bureaucratic bullshit – THAT will be what impresses your future employers the most.

The average cost to attend college for four years is more than $100,000.

If a person can get the degree without being saddled with debt, I think it is well worth it. But if the only way to get that degree is to take on that much debt, I think you should pass. That much debt will lock you into the rat race for a very long time.

On the one hand, I hear from dozens of elderly people, with land, looking for somebody industrious to pass their property to when they die. On the other hand, I have almost as many young people asking me what permaculture college they should go to, or what they should do to pursue permaculture and homesteading if they don't go to college.

Chapter 3

The Impossible Problem and the Simple Solution

Suppose we have an 18-year-old fella named Ferd and Mike is still alive and well. Ferd and Mike have reached an agreement and Ferd is going to live at Mike's and learn "all the things."

I suspect that it won't work out. Mike is willing to teach, but Ferd will need more guidance and hand-holding than Mike is comfortable with or able to give. Ferd wants a guarantee he'll eventually receive the land before heading to Mike's place. Mike won't give that guarantee until he can be sure that Ferd will be some flavor of productive. Even if Ferd takes the risk and comes out, it could take years until Mike is satisfied, and it will probably be less than three months before Ferd moves on, either by his choice or Mike's.

If, instead, Ferd gets a four-year permaculture degree, he will need to find ways to pay the student loans. The average bachelor's degree holder takes 21 years to pay off his or her loans. During all those years of school and repayment Ferd will have done a lot of work, hopefully much of it in the area of permaculture design and consultation. Yet that still doesn't display a sufficient level of practical homesteading worthiness by Mike's standards.

The relationship between Mike and Ferd can work, but there is something missing.

There are millions of people willing to pass their land to somebody worthy (permies.com/t/167533).

There are millions of people wishing to earn a living with their own land, but they don't have land. They might even have the skills to pull it off, but without some way to verify their skills, and without some willing relative, their only choice is to find a way to buy the land themselves. For those who have no skills or are not-quite-fully-skilled, there is still a need to gain that experience. And to complicate things further, they don't even know what skills they need!

The Solution is Simple - SKIP

SKIP is an attempt to make the relationship between Mike and Ferd rock solid, even if they have never met. Mike would be willing to change his will before Ferd arrives. Mike would also be willing to allow Ferd to move onto his land while he is still alive. Ferd knows what to do and how to do it – he has nearly all of the education he will need. Ferd will be self-sufficient upon arrival and will not need to be paid for what he is about to do.

SKIP is nothing more than a list of standardized experiences. Online proof that you did these things – usually pictures and short videos. That's it.

The operational styles of universities were set up well before the internet and digital cameras. SKIP is designed to take advantage of the internet and the idea that nearly everybody has a contraption that can take pictures, or video, and post them on the internet. The software is free, the framework is free – we are now ready for thousands of people to start down the road of SKIP certification.

Ferd can complete all the levels of SKIP at his own pace and at little to no cost. It could even be as quick as three years.

Chapter 4

SKIP

PEX

PEP | PED | PEG | PES | PEJ

SKIP (Skills to Inherit Property) is a broad program to connect industrious people with elderly land owners. Sure, this program can be of value for many other things as well (personal growth, getting work, gaining authority, etc.), but connecting these two groups is the primary purpose.

PEX is "Permaculture Experience according to X" and PEP is "Permaculture Experience according to Paul" – so the "X" is replaced with "Paul." Me. The need for this convention came about very early on. People were offering framework suggestions phrased with words like "must" or "required" or "impossible" – in an attempt to make sure that my framework would include every possible desire for every person on earth. There was clearly a need for something to cover all possible climates, all possible philosophies and all possible scenarios. To do all of that would force the project to be about a thousand times bigger. But with "PEX" and "PEP" we can say that PEP is just one philosophy set in just one climate. PEP is just one scenario, leaving room for everything else under thousands of other PEX programs defined by others in the future.

In time, maybe there could be:

- PEW: Some guy named Willie who is keen on massive scale permaculture systems affecting tens of thousands of people in tropical climates
- PEG: Some guy named Geoff, in a subtropical area, who is keen on swales, bananas and jackfruit
- PES: Some guy named Sepp, in a cold climate, who is is keen on terraces, pigs, aquaculture and root cellars
- PEB: Some guy named Ben, who is heavily into woodland stuff in a cold coastal climate
- PER: Some gal named Raven, who is really into textiles, sheep, and grains in a cool, coastal climate
- PEAS: Some guy named Allan S. who is keen on large scale paddock shift systems as a form of reversing desertification
- PEJ: Some guy named Jean, who is keen on profitable small market gardening in a cold climate
- PEM: Some gal named Maddy, who converts abandoned industrial areas into giant public gardens in cold coastal climates

9

Maybe in 20 years there will be 80 different PEX programs.

Each PEX program can have its own set of requirements – loaded with the values, scenarios and climate that each creator believes is best.

SKIP contains all of the PEXes and the many types of relationships that can happen. SKIP also has information on how relationships can form between the industrious individual and the elderly land owner. SKIP can also have room for different types of legal arrangements, such as shared documentation and incubation for how to manage and grow the future of SKIP and the PEXes.

Because there is a flexible framework for growth, I can now focus on creating a program that I think has value in the Rocky Mountains of Montana – according to my own idea of permaculture. PEP! I can add in things for rocket mass heaters, hugelkultur, round wood timber framing, foraging, passive income streams and community living.

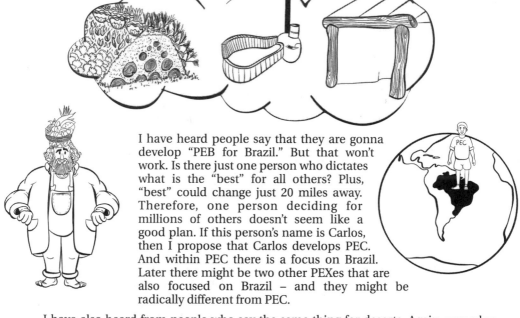

I have heard people say that they are gonna develop "PEB for Brazil." But that won't work. Is there just one person who dictates what is the "best" for all others? Plus, "best" could change just 20 miles away. Therefore, one person deciding for millions of others doesn't seem like a good plan. If this person's name is Carlos, then I propose that Carlos develops PEC. And within PEC there is a focus on Brazil. Later there might be two other PEXes that are also focused on Brazil – and they might be radically different from PEC.

I have also heard from people who say the same thing for deserts. Again, someday there could be dozens of PEXes for deserts. Or urban stuff. Or broadacre. Or jungle. The core concept is that each PEX is tied to one person.

As long as we are expanding our vocabulary, this might be a good time to point out that we have gotten into the habit of calling the industrious people SKIPpers or sometimes PEPpers. Connecting them with an elderly landowner is the next step…

SKIPpers   PEPpers

10

Chapter 5

Otis is a guy who I made up. He is a mish-mash of several dozen people who I have talked to over the years.

Otis has two houses on a 200 acre property. He was born in the old house and he built the newer house himself about 40 years ago.

Otis has three kids. They moved away more than 40 years ago. They are not interested in working this land. They are, however, very interested in inheriting the land and selling it.

Otis knows his time is coming and he wishes that he could will his land to somebody industrious. Somebody who would do more great things with it. Otis knows of some industrious people – but they already have land, so they would just sell this property, no different than his kids.

Otis has the 200 acres, two houses, a good barn and a dozen outbuildings. He has a reliable tractor, a reliable truck and about $80,000 in the bank. He had to let the animals go because he couldn't really care for them properly anymore.

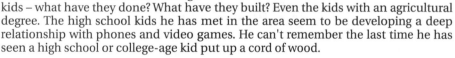

He has put a lot of thought into willing his land to somebody industrious. He doesn't trust college kids – what have they done? What have they built? Even the kids with an agricultural degree. The high school kids he has met in the area seem to be developing a deep relationship with phones and video games. He can't remember the last time he has seen a high school or college-age kid put up a cord of wood.

There are some kids in the local 4-H club, but once they get into high school he doesn't see as much of them anymore. He's not sure if they are still following this path or if they've moved on to something else.

Otis is willing to leave all of his possessions to somebody who is industrious – if he can be certain they are truly industrious. But he can't find that person, so he's giving up. He will just let everything go to his kids. His life's work will be sold to the highest bidder so his kids can have more money.

The Otis Test

For a lot of PEP stuff, I am trying to satisfy many things. And one of those things is "Do I think Otis will be impressed?"

I can see Otis getting online and seeing a list of 12 people who are PEP4 certified (the highest level) and looking for what they will do next. And there is a list of 12 more who will probably be PEP4 certified in the next six months. He needs to see evidence that they have done some real work – according to the standards of Otis. For any one person there is a list of what they have accomplished. And he can see pictures of them doing it and the final product.

PEP4 certification means that they built their own house with their own hands and lived in that house through a Montana winter. They have grown and preserved enough food to feed themselves and several others for a full year. They have put up firewood, sharpened tools and built furniture. They even have a lot of experience with plumbing, electrical, welding, excavators and a whole bunch of interesting stuff Otis has never heard of (that stuff must be good stuff, because dozens of people appear to have experience with it).

Otis needed one person and found two dozen. Success.

Completing four years of PEP is no guarantee of getting Otis's property. But I am certain that there are millions of Otises who are looking to will their land to somebody with the experience gained by completing PEP4.

I actually worry more about the opposite problem: People not finishing all of PEP because an Otis determined they were already good enough.

I suspect that ten years from now, there will be forty Otises for every person actively pursuing four years of PEP.

12

Flavors of Otis

"Otis" is a creation made from dozens of people I have talked to. Years later we now toss the word "Otis" about willy nilly to represent a huge collection of people who wish to develop some sort of relationship with people who have proven themselves to be industrious through the SKIP program.

While we still have a healthy parade of people with land looking for whom they will pass it on to, we are also hearing from:

- people with land that they wish to be cared for while they hold down a career in the city
- people with land who wish to share that land with somebody industrious
- people with land who wish to hire industrious people to work that land
- people with land looking for industrious business partners
- people with land who need to sell it and are willing to sell it for a fraction of the price to somebody who is industrious
- people with events seeking speakers, presenters or teachers
- people in the city with a lot of coin regretting that they never homesteaded – wishing to direct that coin to somebody who will be industrious on a homestead
- people with assets choosing to direct those assets to somebody industrious rather than hold an auction
- people with a pole shed full of stuff that needs to go away, wishing to find someone industrious to haul it away and use it

Years ago my brother met a new widow. Her late husband was 80 and had collected thousands of dollars worth of tools and materials over many decades. Apparently, she did not want to look in his shop because it made her too sad. And she didn't want it auctioned. Nor did she want a pawn shop guy to buy it. Through my brother, she asked if she could just give it all to me (a person she did not know). So I ended up with a mountain of tools and materials. I think there were about 20 buckets full of nuts and bolts. There was a first class tap and die set. Oh sure, there were a half dozen broken lamps and some stuff I didn't need – but I decided that the respectful thing to do was that none of it would go to the dump for at least ten years – I would try to find a use for it. And I did. I ended up using more than a hundred weird things in all sorts of weird ways. Not only has this sort of thing happened to me several times, but I've met dozens of people who received similar gifts over the years. The people giving this stuff just want to know that it will be appreciated and respected. As opposed to a quarter of it being sold and the rest dropped off at the dump.

I suspect that there are (and will be) millions of widows and widowers like this. All these folks need is to have a feeling that the person receiving the gift will appreciate it and authentically use it.

Might you be an Otis???

The SKIP program is a framework for people to learn stuff. But, it is not a framework for people to learn stuff.

Yes, I just stated the opposite thing.

SKIP is a framework for clearly documenting what you have learned – in a way that leans on modern technology (phones with cameras and the internet) and impresses "Otis."

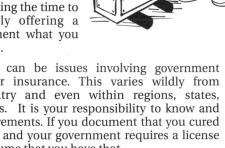

SKIP is not a framework for telling you HOW to do each thing. Or what you need to learn to do a job well. It does not document that you watched 47 YouTube videos to learn how to make soup. Nor does it document that you spent two years at the Cordon Bleau school in Paris to learn how to make soup. Nor does it document you trying to make soup freestyle – wild ass guessing (I bet it could use more salt!). Nor does this framework ensure you took a two week safety course on operating a stovetop. Nor does this framework verify that you wore safety glasses, hearing protection, a helmet and a hazmat suit while making soup.

When you are wildcrafting, YOU need to know the difference between an edible food plant and a toxic plant. It is up to YOU to harvest the right thing. We made the SKIP program free because we are NOT taking the time to teach anything. We are simply offering a framework to document what you have accomplished.

Sometimes there can be issues involving government regulation and/or insurance. This varies wildly from country to country and even within regions, states, counties and cities. It is your responsibility to know and satisfy those requirements. If you document that you cured cancer within SKIP, and your government requires a license and insurance, we assume that you have that.

The SKIP framework is about documenting what you have done. In that sense, the SKIP framework offers structure, motivation, and reward. But the complete education on how to get there is up to you. Some people learn through YouTube videos, and some people learn through classes. Some people learn through podcasts and others through articles or books. Some people can teach themselves. Some people already know this stuff, and the SKIP framework will simply be a way for them to demonstrate what they already know. There are thousands of possible paths to getting any one badge.

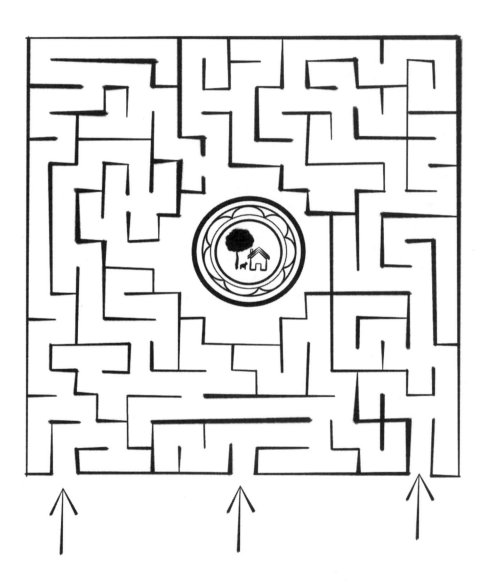

Good luck. Work hard. Be safe. Live large.

15

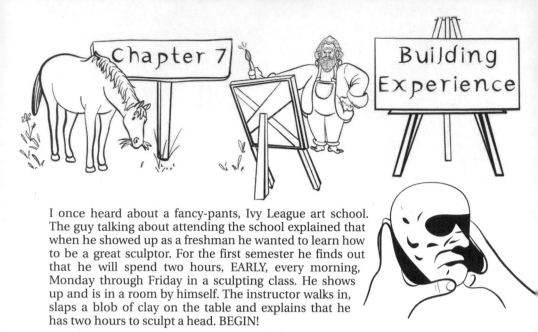

I once heard about a fancy-pants, Ivy League art school. The guy talking about attending the school explained that when he showed up as a freshman he wanted to learn how to be a great sculptor. For the first semester he finds out that he will spend two hours, EARLY, every morning, Monday through Friday in a sculpting class. He shows up and is in a room by himself. The instructor walks in, slaps a blob of clay on the table and explains that he has two hours to sculpt a head. BEGIN!

At the end of the two hours, he thinks he has done a reasonably good job for his first day – especially given only two hours. The instructor comes back into the room and smashes it. "See you tomorrow."

The next day: "You have two hours to sculpt a head."
Two hours. Smash.

Wednesday: smash.

Thursday: smash.

It's like he isn't even looking at it.
He doesn't give any feedback.

Day after day: smash.

For four years, two hours a day, Monday through Friday: sculpt a head and smash.

The guy telling the story explains that at the end of the four years, the heads he could sculpt in two hours were rather magnificent. It is a pity they were all smashed.

A long time ago I had a thousand things rattling around in my brain that needed to be put to paper. Ideas that could not be conveyed with the English language. So I took a drawing class. On the first day of class, the instructor showed us his amazing drawing skills. So magnificent! And he did it so fast!

He said there was nothing he could teach us. Learning to draw is 100% experience. You just sit down with paper and a pencil and draw. Call it doodling if you want. The more you draw, the better you get. If you become obsessed with drawing and spend fifteen hours a day drawing, then you can probably get some stuff published in a couple of months. If you spend an hour a day drawing, that point might come in a few years. He was emphatic that no amount of teaching or advice would change any of that. The only thing a teacher can do is to get you to spend some time drawing instead of doing something else. So, that's what the class was going to do.

And that is what we did.

When it comes to homesteading and permaculture, I think the repetitive experiences get you a long way towards general competence. Not 100% but a good 70%. It helps to know about different tools and techniques. But… 70% is a lot.

There is a lot to be said for "wax on, wax off."

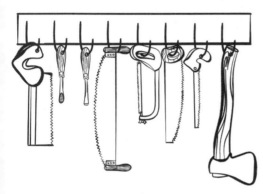

The ceramics teacher announced on opening day that he was dividing the class into two groups. All those on the left side of the studio, he said, would be graded solely on the quantity of work they produced, all those on the right solely on its quality.

His procedure was simple: on the final day of class he would bring in his bathroom scales and weigh the work of the "quantity" group: fifty pound of pots rated an "A", forty pounds a "B", and so on. Those being graded on "quality", however, needed to produce only one pot – albeit a perfect one – to get an "A".

Well, came grading time and a curious fact emerged: the works of highest quality were all produced by the group being graded for quantity. It seems that while the "quantity" group was busily churning out piles of work – and learning from their mistakes – the "quality" group had sat theorizing about perfection, and in the end had little more to show for their efforts than grandiose theories and a pile of dead clay.

-Art and Fear (David Bayles and Ted Orland)

"Anything worth doing well,
is worth doing poorly first"

- Joel Salatin

I went to college and then got a job. It took me a long time to pay off my student loans and then I worked extra hard to get the money to buy a homestead. I kept working in order to buy a tractor… and some stuff to connect to the tractor… and put in a new septic tank drain field… and animals and trees and feed and tools and on and on and on. And then I started meeting old geezers looking for somebody to will their homestead to – somebody who would keep their homestead going with cool homestead stuff. Several of them offered their homestead to me! I wish I knew about these people before I started college!

College is widely recognized as the best path to a high paying career. The average time it takes to pay off student loan debt is 21.1 years (credible.com). Add in a homestead and a 30 year mortgage and PRESTO – the average person is ready to retire after about 40 years. Pretty predictable because this is a well worn path. If you work extra hard, live freaky cheap, and have a bit of luck, you might be able to carve ten years off of that.

I'd like to propose SKIP as an alternative to college. The SKIP path doesn't help you get a high paying career, but it eliminates the need for all that high pay. Plus, it gets you to a homestead retirement package much faster.

If your goal is to retire on a homestead, college will get you there in 40 years, and SKIP will get you there in 4 years.

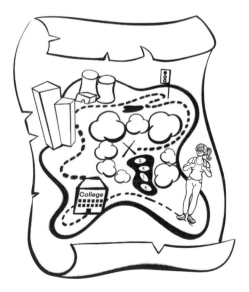

Four years of college	Four years of SKIP
Learn how to be independently productive.	Learn how to be independently productive.
Learn to balance classwork and fun.	Learn to balance accomplishments and fun.
Meet new people and make contacts.	Meet new people and make contacts.
Academic knowledge on the subjects of your choice.	Practical knowledge on the subjects of your choice.
$142,880 on average for a four year college degree.	Limited data so far. Can be utterly free. Some people might pay a few thousand dollars to attend some events each year.
You spend 40 hours a week studying, and if you have time, you can also spend 20 hours a week building a better world.	You spend 40 hours a week building a better world, and if you have time, you can bump that up to 60.
Choosing a major that follows your passions will make college and your career more enjoyable, but it might be a lot longer until you can retire. Choosing a major that will improve your income will make your college days and career less enjoyable, but you can get to retirement faster.	If SKIP aligns with your passions, it will make the four years you pursue it more enjoyable, and then you can retire to a life following your passions.
Four years of peak physical health spent developing a relationship with books and tests.	Four years of peak physical health spent actively building permaculture and homesteading skills.
Probably living in a city in a dorm or apartment for four years.	Probably living in the country for four years.
College courses have a rigid schedule.	SKIP is entirely at your own pace.
Well established system.	Not an established educational path. Possibly a lot more opportunities and choices for early adopters.

ATM
Insufficient funds for withdrawal
$-142,880.00
Cancel   Accept
Bank of Dreams

After college – The rat race	After SKIP – Retired
The workplace can become a living nightmare.	Dodge the concept of "employment" entirely. A flock of chickens are fun to work with, and if the chickens piss you off, you can make soup.
You may not find employment in your chosen field.	Dodge the concept of "employment" entirely. You will always need food and shelter – these skills never become obsolete.
After getting your degree, you might hit a point where you cannot find employment at all.	Dodge the concept of "employment" entirely. Go directly to retirement with a homestead and massive permaculture gardens. You have the skills to eliminate the need for income, and those same skills can also bring in an income if you choose.
Your skills might become obsolete.	You will always need food and shelter– these skills never become obsolete.
You may not get a job when you graduate.	Dodge the concept of "employment" entirely.
Likely destined for a job in a city.	Likely destined for a homestead in the country.
40+ hour work week – probably for 40+ years.	Retired. Part time gardening or animal care.
Likely have a dress code.	Retired people have no dress code.
The average American spends 5 hours per week commuting to their job.	No commute.
Politics, the economy, war… many things beyond your control can threaten your ability to retain employment.	Politics, the economy, war… these things are small and far away when you have a solid home, glorious gardens and homesteading/ permaculture skills.
If the SHTF… you're in a scary situation.	If the SHTF… you are well prepared.

	Quickly master teachable skills in a world yearning for homesteading and permaculture skills. 
Takes years to become an authority on a subject.	
10 years before you can arrange a down payment on a homestead. 25 years before you might own your own homestead debt-free (but not able to retire yet). 40 years before you are able to retire with solid equipment, a solid home and a solid nest egg.	Start with your own homestead debt-free, complete with solid equipment, a solid home and a solid nest egg.

Here's an odd idea: Do the normal college thing and do SKIP on the side. SKIP could fill your summer vacations, spring break, winter vacations and weekends. Maybe you could have a gap year of SKIP. Maybe a bit during high school. And maybe by the time you graduate from college, you will have your choice between a job and a homestead.

When planning your future, one thing we often think about is risk. We often pursue a million dollars because we imagine that having a million dollars will add a lot of safety to our future. But inflation, poor investments or other financial issues can wipe that out quickly. A homestead and the SKIP skills have far more safety than a million dollars.

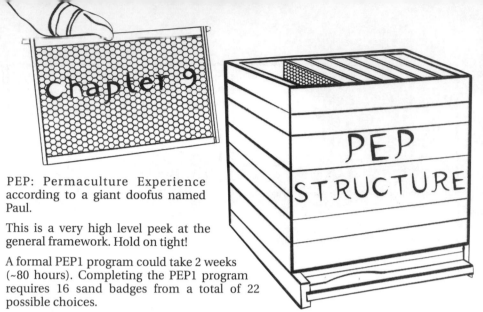

Chapter 9

PEP: Permaculture Experience according to a giant doofus named Paul.

This is a very high level peek at the general framework. Hold on tight!

A formal PEP1 program could take 2 weeks (~80 hours). Completing the PEP1 program requires 16 sand badges from a total of 22 possible choices.

16 sand badges

A formal PEP2 program could fill a summer (~510 hours). It requires 1 wood badge + 7 straw badges + 14 sand badges. At this point, you will have earned at least one sand badge in each of the 22 aspects of PEP.

1 wood badge   7 straw badges   14 sand badges

A formal PEP3 program could take about nine months (~1550 hours). It requires 7 wood badges + 15 straw badges.

15 straw badges

7 wood badges

A formal PEP4 program could take a little over two years (~4700 hours). It requires 3 iron badges + 12 wood badges + 7 straw badges.

3 iron badges   12 wood badges   7 straw badges

The approximate time, in direct experience (excluding learning and documenting), for an excellent student to complete a single badge would be about:

- sand badge: ~5 hours
- straw badge: ~35 more hours, about 4 or 5 days, spread over weeks or months
- wood badge: ~180 more hours, about 4 to 5 weeks, spread out over months or a year
- iron badge: ~1030 more hours, about six months, spread out over a couple years

A few people will complete the PEP1 program in a rather busy two weeks – most people will need three to five weeks. Some people will complete PEP1 without attending any SKIP events. They would have done it all from home – posting pictures of their progress to permies and getting certified on Permies.com.

Here's how it works. Each PEP badge has a webpage on Permies.com, where you will find a variety of Badge Bits (BBs) to choose from. You can follow the BB links to descriptions and requirements for completing each BB. The BB pages are also where you'll submit proof of meeting the BB requirements through descriptions, photos, and/or videos.

When all the required BBs for a PEP badge have been certified, you'll submit a list of links to those BBs on the PEP badge webpage. Once those links are verified, you'll earn the badge! Likewise, after you've completed your first 16 sand badges, you can submit a list of your sand badge links to the PEP1 webpage and become PEP1 certified.

Most people are probably going to work on their straw badge bits only after they have completed their sand badge. And it is perfectly fine to earn BBs in straw, wood or iron before completing your sand badge, BUT you cannot get your straw badge until you have completed your sand badge. The same goes for the wood and iron badges.

Edge Case BBs

This is a free program. Some people post a BB thinking "close enough, it should be fine." But it is not fine because it makes a lot of work for the volunteer certifiers.

If the person doing the certifying can process a dozen certifications quickly, then this is an easy and quick task. But if one of the submissions is an edge case (not quite good enough), or if a submission needs to be rejected, it is no longer an easy and quick task.

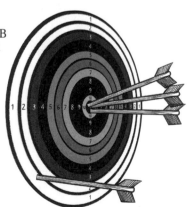

We encountered a problem where people doing the certifying would only process the BBs that were quick and easy leaving the edge cases for others. The edge case BBs would often sit for a week or two before the submitter would complain and after a lot of reluctance somebody would take the time to get it sorted. In the end, edge case BBs were taking 50 times more effort. Edge case BBs were starting to clog our system which would otherwise have worked quite smoothly.

I suppose this could all get quickly sorted out by a paid professional. But we are back to the whole thing being free – so there is no way to pay such a person.

When you submit, please make a PROPER submission meeting ALL of the requirements. This is not something for a "B" grade. There is only "A", "A+" and "F." If you go to submit and realize that you forgot to take a picture at the beginning, you will need to do it over! Please, DO NOT submit and hope it gets through. Please be respectful to the people donating their time to make this work. They are donating their time to help you!

Certifying Others

The PEP program is built on a foundation of self-perpetuation. And it's free! FREE!

In order to get the "free" thing to work, we require people getting higher badges to certify the lower badges. That way, the rigor of the PEP system can be kept up by people who have been publicly verified as having done these tasks before, AND have a keen interest in maintaining our high standards!

To get PEP1 certified, you need to have certified many BBs of others. We built something into our software for this, but so far it has not been an issue – everybody who has reached PEP1 has certified far more BBs than the system required. I like to think that this says something lovely about the people seeking PEP1 certification.

To certify someone else's BB, you need to have earned the Sand badge for that aspect and also completed that BB yourself.

Chapter 10

Permaculture Experience for Apartment Dwellers

Also known as "Permaculture Experience Anywhere."

PEA is a lot like PEP, but we have carefully crafted it to be for people anywhere in the world. Especially people in tiny apartments with a lot of restrictions.

PEA1 does NOT require:

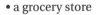

- a balcony
  - a window that opens
  - a park nearby
  - a community garden nearby
  - access to a friend's garden or small farm
- a nail into a wall or ceiling
- permission for pets or animals

The entire PEA program wouldn't be possible without the hard work of D. X. Logan.

We do assume that the person pursuing PEA does have access to:

- a grocery store
- a hardware store
- online retailers like Amazon and Ebay

All badges can be done by vegans and you can get PEA1 certified as a vegan.

We do hope that many people who start with PEA will eventually transition to PEP. Many PEA badges will give you full credit for PEP activities, so you can work on both at the same time!

We have fully defined the sand badges for PEA so that people can get PEA1 certification.

PEA1 requires the same amount of total experience as PEP1 – about 80 hours. PEA1 takes 12 badges to accomplish versus 16 for PEP1. Therefore each PEA badge takes a bit more effort.

Gardening

Use permaculture techniques to grow delicious food. Projects include hugelkultur, chop and drop, Ruth Stout style composting, seed saving, producing large volumes of food, polyculture, starting perennials from seed, food forests...

Natural Building

Build big things. Build experiences with several styles of natural building that work in a cold climate, with the grand finale being a wofati. Techniques: cob, plaster, straw bale, wofati, natural paint, adobe, natural roofing, waterproofing, doors and gates, dry stack foundation, wood ash cement, cob floor, wattle and daub...

Woodland Care

Transition from using a forest to developing a symbiotic relationship with a woodland. Create junkpole fences, firewood, lumber, gin poles, skiddable sheds, rock jacks, berm sheds, living fences and twig construction (arbors, tomato cages, trellises, wattle fence). Cut trees manually and with power tools, peel logs, make roofing shakes, plant tree seeds, plant woodland species, grow edible mushrooms, coppice trees...

Round Wood Woodworking

Build everything from logs, branches, and sticks using zero glue and rarely any metal. Nothing starts with dimensional lumber. Power tools can be okay, but, in general, less power tools. Some projects specify no power tools. Quite a bit of working with green (freshly harvested) wood. Small and large joinery, mixing green wood with dried wood, three log benches, spoon carving, shaving horse, sawhorse, sawbuck, chairs and other roundwood furniture, shrink pot, box from a piece of firewood, pole lathe, bowl from a pole lathe, skiddable shed for green wood woodworking, Proenneke hinge, door latch...

Tool Care

Maintain and repair tools of all sizes. Small tool care (sharpening/handles/etc.), power tool care (chainsaws, saws, drills, power hand tools as well as stationary power tools), large tool care (truck/tractor/ etc.), appliance repair, bicycle repair, build a tool shed, optimize a shop, build a materials shed, create dry places to park/charge large equipment...

Earthworks

Use large equipment to make dramatic changes to the landscape. Build roads, trails, terraces, ponds, berms, ditches, prepare building sites, natural swimming pools, dry stack, passive garden heaters, garden ATI (Annualized Thermal Inertia)...

Dimensional Lumber Woodworking

Includes construction, cabinetry and fine woodworking. No plywood, waferboard or particle board. Power tools, nails and screws are used, but hopefully less than in most construction. This badge has a strong emphasis on good joinery over more fasteners. Projects include: bird houses, laying deck, shelves, wooden toolbox, stool, box, picnic table, wood bucket, skiddable lumber storage shed, porta cabin...

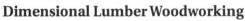

Rocket

Build and maintain wood burning contraptions that cut energy and wood use by 90%. Build and become proficient at: rocket mass heaters, rocket ovens, rocket cooktops, rocket water heaters, outdoor kitchens...

Food Prep and Preservation

Make delicious food using energy saving methods like hay box cooking, rocket ovens and solar dehydrators. Skills include cooking, boiling, baking, frying, cast iron care, and preserving the harvest with canning, drying, pickling and fermenting...

Animal Care

Sand and straw badges are vegan friendly. Care for domestic animals and provide resources and infrastructure to encourage wild animals to your mutual benefit. Domestic animal care includes keeping chickens, pigs, cattle, rabbits, sheep, goats, bees, and fish, as well as butchering, honey production and dairy production.

Wildlife care includes building homes for birds, bats, pollinators, garden-friendly insects, snakes, lizards…

Foraging

Harvest and preserve food from the wild. Gather fresh fruits, berries, nuts, greens, mushrooms, and vegetables from wild sources. Practice fishing and hunting (with vegan alternatives) respectfully. Enhance the harvest with some forage gardening.

Community Living

Build a desirable community and create community experiences with others. Skills include creating public art, cooking meals for a group, leading workshops and presentations, improving a common space, creating a community holiday, creating a LIC (labor investment collective), giving tours, creating a map, organizing community events…

Textiles

Make clothing and other useful textiles. Skills include mending, weaving, knitting, crochet, spinning, sewing, leatherwork, and basketry. This aspect also includes growing and harvesting the materials to make you own clothes! Tasks include making curtains, shoes, upholstered furniture, tents, yurts…

Greywater and Willow Feeders

There is no "waste" in nature. Horticultural techniques for safe management of poop, pee and greywater. Use soaps and cleaners that are greywater friendly and reuse wash water in the garden. Plant "poop beasts" like willow, poplar and cottonwood. Proper handling of "willow candy." Build mulch pits and "willow feeders."

Metalworking

Build and repair metal things. Welding, cutting, blacksmithing, casting, bending/shaping, and grinding. Large farm equipment as well as small projects.

Plumbing and Hot Water

 Pressurized and non-pressurized systems. Installing, replacing, or repairing pipes. Maintain and build new systems. Stop leaks, maintain hoses, repair or replace drains, toilets, faucets, garden hydrants, wells...

Electricity

Maintain and build electrical systems including AC (alternating current) and DC (direct current) as well as on grid and off grid. Battery maintenance, install outlets, breaker panels, repair and build solar systems...

Commerce

 Prove that you can earn money in multiple ways, including some that are non-conventional. Prove to Otis that you would arrive with your own income streams and would not be dependent on his savings. Demonstrate: several income models over the internet, passive income streams, earning money through permaculture labor and cottage industries...

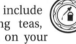

Natural Medicine

Harvest healing herbs from a garden and the wild to establish a collection of medicines. Skills include identifying plants and their properties, making teas, tinctures, oils, salves, poultices and using them on your friends.

Nest

 Demonstrate to Otis that if you stay in his second house, you'll take care of it. Cleaning, shovelling snow, doing laundry, simple house maintenance, and other daily, repetitive tasks that make your living space liveable according to the standards of Otis.

Homesteading

 Known experiences that don't fit into the other aspects. Backing up a trailer, plowing snow, rockjacks, scything, removing snow from a roof, moving outbuildings, adding onto an existing house...

Oddball

 Unpredictable, unique and creative experiences worthy of PEP. Rather than BBs, this aspect has a point system to earn badges.

29

Chapter 12

The 16 Aspects of PEA

Gardening

This badge starts with the idea of growing food, in pots, inside of an apartment. Some things will do better in this respect than others – and we found some winners! But we also add in some seed saving, a mushroom kit, a worm bin (for fertilizer!) and some general houseplant tasks. Let's turn your apartment into a permaculture jungle!

Round Wood Woodworking

Rather than send you off into the wild to get wood, we expect an apartment dweller to start with a purchased blank or to purchase some raw materials on eBay. Carve a spoon, whittle a couple of mallets, make some more kitchen tools and maybe a chess set that's a "bit rough, but good enough."

Toolcare

Sharpen some knives, a hand saw, a pair of scissors and a chisel. Bring an old hand tool back to life and repair a kitchen appliance.

Dimensional Lumber Woodworking

We have come up with projects that don't need hammering or a table saw. Things that can be built quietly. A stool, a shelf, a wood box, wood-burned artwork and a toolbox.

Food Prep and Preservation

Many of the same things in PEP, but without the rocket and solar stuff. You still have cast iron care, fermenting, pickling, canning and drying food. Then some good old fashioned cooking: a stir fry, some pizza, bread, condiments and cheese (vegan cheese if you want).

Animal Care

We start with the assumption that you are not allowed to have pets. But some people might be allowed to have an aquarium. With that thought we decided to run with a points system. A points system makes it so the people with the most restrictive rules can still get the badge done (deal with pest problems, build things that will be installed elsewhere, etc.), and people with looser rules can do some things that are a bit more fun (aquarium, vermicomposting, guinea pigs, black soldier fly larvae, silkworms, quail, etc.).

Foraging

Maybe 60% of foraging is being able to recognize what the plant looks like and having some idea what to do with it when you have it. We got the idea that you could buy the plant and that by cooking with this unusual plant, you would become more familiar with it. It isn't as good as being out in the wild, but it does make you much better prepared for when that day might come. Perhaps a bit of stinging nettle tea? Or maybe make a soup with dandelions. How about some huckleberry pie!

Community Living

Build skills to build community – for anybody within a small apartment. For some this is easy, and for others, this will be one badge that they don't do. Host a meal for eight people, create public art, get a roommate, or do any of the PEP community BBs.

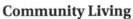

Textiles

It turns out that everything in the PEP sand badge can be done in any apartment! Easy peasy! And we added a sewing kit, a button jar and a couple other simple things.

Greywater

We are confident that all landlords would object to major plumbing changes. Instead, we have a list of a dozen simple things you can do (of which, you only need to do eight) in any apartment. Place a small, soft bucket in the shower and re-use that water; use a dishpan; experiment with water filters, and go poo-less!

Metalworking

Start with projects that will convert a pop can into something useful. Then a wire coat hanger. Then you choose between projects that might include: upcycling a spoon, soldering a trivet from copper pipe, turn a box end wrench into a spoon carving knife… dozens of projects to choose from, all of which can be done without welding, firing up a power grinder or mounting something to a wall.

Electricity

Most apartment dwellers will not be allowed to modify the wiring in their apartment, but they can create some simple electrical appliances like a lamp! There are a few BBs for dabbling with solar and rechargeable batteries. And for testing your existing appliances to develop a strategy to cut your energy usage by 30% or more.

Commerce

Prove that you are capable of earning money anywhere in the world. You will develop a small residual income stream that will continue to pay you over the years to come without any further effort. You will also sell products and services in a way that does not require you to leave your apartment.

Natural Medicine

90% of the experience is with acquiring the ingredients and following the proper steps. If you were on a homestead, you would probably grow or forage most of these ingredients, but for PEA we simply require that you "acquire" the ingredients – probably purchase. Dry some fresh ingredients for tea, create a vinegar infusion, an oil infusion, a salve, a tincture, a poultice, a syrup, and a decoction.

Nest

Most of these things you probably already do. But we want to push your boundaries a little by focusing on tasks that eliminate common household toxins. Wash clothes by hand, grease hinges, oil your kitchen woods, whiten clothes without bleach, and clean with edible cleaners.

Oddball

Exactly the same as PEP. You have your own fascinating projects that fall within the standards of PEX. Things that we didn't think to list here, or opportunities that presented themselves to you. Probably some sort of repair, but it could also be a creative creation.

Chapter 13

There are thousands of gardening techniques. And hundreds of climates, soil types and challenges for each different region.

Thanks to Shawn Klassen-Koop for putting a lot of effort into all of the sand badges for all of PEP – especially shaping all of the gardening badges.

When homesteading, Joel Salatin tells us that many people give up because somebody else has an unfair advantage. **Joel asks us to create our own unfair advantage.**

Hugelkultur is a gardening technique that is a lot of work up front, followed by a lot of reward down the road. Your food systems become more resilient and the flavor of your food becomes much better. Less work, better food.

Featured Sand Badge BB: Build a Hugelkultur

Show Otis you have the gumption to put the effort in now so you can reap the reward later.

Sprinkle of wood, sprinkle of soil, repeat...

Jump into the full power of permaculture gardening. Create a garden that will pump out food for decades with no further effort.

Minimum requirements:
- 7 feet tall, 7 feet wide, 6 feet long
- Mulch it with at least 4 different kinds of mulch
- Seed/plant at least a dozen different species
- Mostly nitrogen fixers
- At least three comfrey plants
- At least three sunchokes
- At least a dozen Sepp Holzer grains

Clarifications:
- You may use an excavator or other heavy equipment if desired (opportunity for a two-fer with the earthworks badge)
- If you dig 3 foot deep trenches on either side of the hugelkultur spot, you can use that soil, mixed with wood, to make a hugelkultur bed that is 4 feet above grade but 7 feet tall relative to the bottom of the trench
- If you are building on a slope, measure the height from both sides and the average needs to be 7 feet or higher

Provide proof of the following as pictures or video (<2 mins):
- Two views of the site before the work is started with the intended location marked out
  - Probably marked with wood laid on the ground that will soon be buried!
- Three views of different stages of construction, showing the contents of the hugelkultur
- One view when the hugelkultur is completely built but not planted or mulched proving it is 7 feet tall and 6 feet long
- All the stuff about to be planted
- A paragraph or two of what wood was used and where it came from, what was planted, what mulches were applied and anything else interesting
- Two views of the site after the work is completed from the same two locations as at the beginning

33

Sand badge
- ☐ Build a hugelkultur 7 feet tall and 6 feet long
- ☐ Chop and drop (50 square feet)
- ☐ Ruth Stout style composting (2 spots)

- ☐ Seed saving
- ☐ Encourage volunteer or wild plants
  (probably mulching or chop and drop)
    - ☐ Grow and harvest 100,000 calories
      - From at least 12 species
    - ☐ Build a hugelkultur 7 feet tall and 12 feet long
- ☐ Direct seed perennials

Straw badge

Wood badge
- ☐ Grow and harvest 1 million calories
  - From at least 30 species
  - All systems are polyculture systems
- ☐ Build a ¼ acre food forest
- ☐ Grow perennials from seed
- ☐ Build a hugelkultur 7 feet tall and 24 feet long

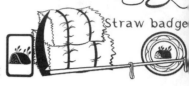

Iron badge
- ☐ Grow and harvest 4 million calories in one year
  - From at least 30 species
  - All systems are polyculture systems
- ☐ Build hugelkultur 7 feet tall
  - Total of 150 feet long
  - At least six beds
- ☐ Harvest fruit from 12 trees that you started from seed
- ☐ Build a 1 acre food forest
  - Sun scoop shape
  - No frost pocket
  - Covers at least an acre
  - Full seven layers
- ☐ Landrace seed saving (at least 12 species for at least 3 generations)

Sample Sand Badge BB: Chop and Drop

Chop and drop is a technique where you cut unwanted plants and use the cuttings as a smothering mulch on other unwanted plants while simultaneously mulching around desired plants.

Usually, 3 square feet of area would be chopped to fully smother/mulch 1 square foot.

Minimum requirements:
- Chop materials and mulch 50 square feet of desirable plants

Provide proof of the following as pictures or video (<2 mins):
- The area prior to mulching
- After mulching

Clarifications:
- You may chop material from another area if needed

Sample Sand Badge BB: Ruth Stout Style Composting

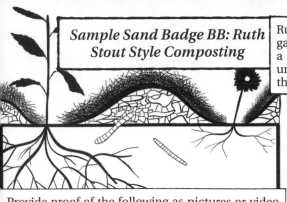

Ruth Stout heavily mulched her gardens. Instead of putting scraps in a compost pile, tuck them in or under your mulch to directly feed the soil.

Provide proof of the following as pictures or video (<2 mins):

- The bucket of kitchen scraps next to the opened mulch
- The empty bucket and the new mound of mulch
- Repeat for the second bucket
- Describe the volume of your bucket(s) and how full they were

Minimum requirements:

- Start with two areas that have already been mulched (or mulch two places)
- Collect two 5 gallon buckets of kitchen scraps
- Open a spot in the mulch for the kitchen scraps
- Plop one bucket of kitchen scraps in a spot so that the material will not touch desirable plants
- Cover the kitchen scraps with existing mulch or new mulch
- Repeat in another spot for second bucket

Clarifications:

- If you collect food scraps in smaller quantities it's fine to do more buckets that are smaller as long as they add up to 10 gallons

Sample Straw Badge BB: Grow and Harvest 100,000 Calories

An average person needs one million calories per year. So this BB is for proving that you can grow one tenth of the average person's food needs.

Minimum requirements:

- Grow, harvest and use 12 or more species (except in cases where species are quite different as in the brassica family) totaling 100,000 calories
- Minimum of 2,000 calories from each of the 12 species
- Perennials, biennials and annuals are fine but foraging is not
- Can not be used for animal feed
- No inputs from more than 500 feet away (tomato starts from the big box store aren't allowed) except for seeds
- This can be completed over a series of growing seasons (please just one submission when you are complete)

To put it in perspective, there are 10,000 calories in:

- 35 pounds of potatoes
- 10 pounds of prunes
- 40 quarts of salsa
- 6 pounds of dried strawberries
- 55 pounds of onions
- 50 pounds of winter squash
- 30 pounds of sunchokes
- 7 pounds of field corn or rye or most grains
- 7 pounds of dried black beans
- 4 pounds of whole sunflower seeds

Clarifications:

- Seed potatoes (or tubers or slips) are allowed provided that you show at least five times more final produce than the "seed"

Provide proof of the following as pictures or video (<2 mins):

- Each of the 12+ species of food at harvest or in storage (whichever is most applicable to prove you did it)
- Detail the weight of each species and how many calories it represents
- Place(s) where your food is growing

35

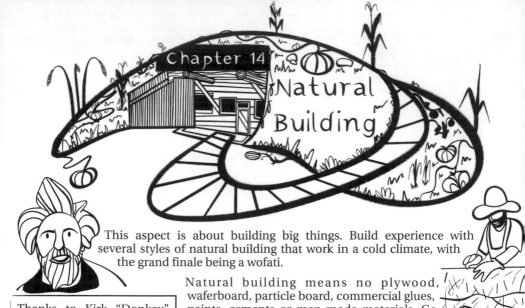

Chapter 14

Natural Building

This aspect is about building big things. Build experience with several styles of natural building that work in a cold climate, with the grand finale being a wofati.

Natural building means no plywood, waferboard, particle board, commercial glues, paints, cements or man-made materials. Go easy on the dimensional lumber and fasteners.

Thanks to Kirk "Donkey" Mobert for developing a lot of substance for this aspect.

Lots of round wood timber framing, cob, dry stack rock, straw bale, clay based paints, adobe, linseed oil, slip straw…

Featured Sand Badge BB: Create 12 Adobe Bricks

Adobe bricks are essentially cob building blocks, where a large portion of the drying time (which can be significant) is done before the building process begins. They can be used to build a large list of items very quickly, including RMHs, built-in furniture, ovens and even whole houses.

To make adobe bricks you need an adobe form. Typically a wood frame, open at the top and bottom for forming cob into bricks. Wet the adobe form by dipping it in water, place it on bare ground and toss in a wet-ish cob mix (literally tossing in handfuls, throwing it down hard will eliminate air pockets). Level the mix off to the top of the form, then pull the form away, leaving the wet brick behind. Wet the form between bricks. Repeat. When dry enough to move without deforming, flip the bricks on their narrow edge to finish drying.

Minimum requirements:
• Make 12 bricks
• 12 by 6 by 3 inches

Provide proof of the following as pictures or video (<2 mins):
• Show your mix and tools
• Action shot
• Bricks drying on edge

36

Lloyd list - complete 3:
☐ Create 12 adobe bricks
☐ Make a natural paint and paint a 4x8 foot area
☐ Make white wash and use it on a 4x8 foot area
☐ Use low grade cob to fill between logs in a wofati – 20 linear feet
☐ Create a rock foundation under a skiddable structure to level the structure
☐ Add 25 square feet of roof (cedar shakes or similar style of wood roof) to a structure

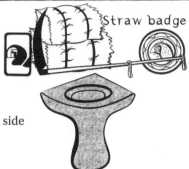

Complete all the BBs in the "Lloyd list"
☐ Find and assess clay sub-soil for making cob/adobe bricks, try different mixes, keep notes, test them to destruction (smash with hammer, toss in fire, etc.), choose best mixes
☐ Build a tiny shed on skids
  • 6 feet wide, 3 feet deep, holds garbage cans and some tools and has a bench on the back side
☐ Build a cob sink

Donkey list - complete 2:
☐ Tree stand
☐ Build a solar finder, locate true solar south and leave a permanent marker
☐ Hang a door using handmade wooden hinges
☐ Build garden gate from found or harvested objects
☐ Earth plaster a wall, with varying patterns and color
  • Minimum of 7 feet tall, 10 feet long, at least 2 colors and you made the plaster/paints
  ☐ Dirt and linseed oil floor
  ☐ Slip straw wall
    • Must be minimum 7 feet tall by 8 feet long by 8 inches thick
  ☐ Build short, dry stack rock foundation
  ☐ Build adobe brick and cob bench
    • 2 butts wide minimum
  ☐ Clay paint a room or rooms
    • Make the paint and cover a minimum of 80 linear feet of wall

Finish the Donkey list
☐ Build an operating window, including the frame, from scratch
☐ Straw bale wall in a wofati
☐ Home made wood ash cement
  • Build one of the following:
    - 5 gallon plant pot
    - 5 gallon water trough
    - Combination bird bath and insect watering station
    - 3 flow form water aerators

☐ Build freezer wofati
- At least 100 square feet of freezer space and at least 100 square feet of root cellar space
- Completing the Roundwood Iron badge freezer wofati BB would meet this requirement

Complete One:
☐ Cob floor
☐ Wattle and daub wall for a berm shed
☐ Lime plaster a wall or set of walls
☐ Tree house
- Must be at least 10 feet off the ground, 70 square feet and have 7 feet of head clearance

☐ Build a cob bench with a round pole construction roof.
☐ Build adobe doghouse (or faerie house) with Nubian vault roof
　　☐ Cob sun trap
　　　- Wall is at least 15 linear feet, height at least 6 feet, arched pass through with door or gate
　　☐ A piece of an outdoor classroom with a Rumford fireplace

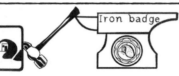

☐ Build a wofati and live in it for a winter
- Minimum of 200 square feet interior.
- Structure must be 100% complete by October 15. "Live in it for a winter" means October 15 to March 20 with being gone for no more than 7 days.

Sample Sand Badge BB: Make and use natural paint

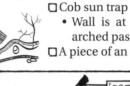

Clay paints are a simple, inexpensive, effective and beautiful way to finish, color and freshen homes or just about any built environment.

Provide proof of the following as pictures or video (<2 mins):
- Raw materials. Your clay rich subsoil, other paint ingredients and the tools you used
- Action pic
- Image of the final result

Minimum requirements:
- Make natural paint from clay and similar natural materials
- Use it on a 4x8 foot area

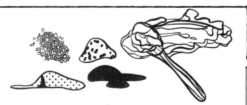

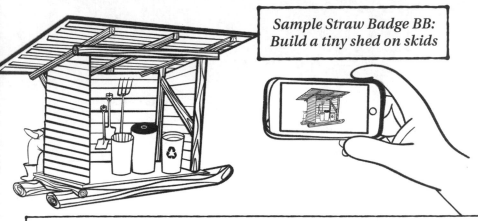

Sample Straw Badge BB:
Build a tiny shed on skids

When you're improving a homestead, you often end up building structures for various needs. If only you could build one structure that could be a bit flexible and handle different jobs. Or change its purpose when the opportunity presents itself. You can! I give you... The Skiddable Structure!

You're building a somewhat normal structure, it's just built on top of two beefy skids. Then you can hook it up to a tractor, or team of horses, or a big group of friends, and move it to a new location. The construction of the skids is important, as are the connection points for the tractor. So, practice on a small structure first – Like a tiny shed!

The one requirement that may seem out of place is the bench. Having lots of shady places to sit and chat is helpful in sunny Montana. You can build a bench and put it under a tree but it will still get wet. By building it into your tiny shed you will always have a somewhat protected area to sit a spell.

Minimum requirements:
- 6 feet wide, 3 feet deep and 6 feet interior height
- Hold one garbage can
- Hold one sand barrel (for winter traction)
- Hold one recycling can
- Maybe a shovel or two
- Maybe offer power and/or water
- Has a bench built in to the back side so people can sit under the roof

Provide proof of the following as pictures or video (<2 mins):
- The wood you're starting with
- The skids and framework assembled
- The construction about 60% to 90% complete
- The finished structure from a few angles

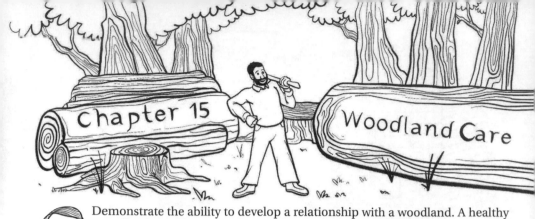

Chapter 15 — Woodland Care

Demonstrate the ability to develop a relationship with a woodland. A healthy woodland is diverse and provides building materials, food, fuel and something that builds your soul. Conventional forestry is cash focused and tends to transform the soil into lifeless dirt.

Otis has met too many people who can't even put up a single cord of firewood – and this is his primary metric. How many cords of firewood can you put up in a day? Experience with a sawmill or cleaving shakes is a bonus!

Thanks to Steve Thorn for developing a lot of substance for this aspect.

I think that woodland care is often about prepping materials. To be a sort of permaculture "Home Depot" for other projects.

Featured Sand Badge BB:
Peel two trees and put up off the ground to dry

These two trees are most likely the trees dropped in another BB.

Peeling a tree means removing the bark and cambium layer of a tree after limbing it. This helps it dry faster, be less prone to rot, and be ready for woodworking.

This is easier on smaller trees and can possibly be done with a large knife. On larger trees, a draw knife or bark spud will be quicker.

Harvested live trees make great material for building things in the Round Wood Woodworking PEP badge!

Do not wrap the logs, they need air movement. Some people cobble together something roof-like over the logs. That can help, but only if there is plenty of air space between the logs and roof, plus zero wall-like things. Lots of air can still move through. In Montana, leaving the logs uncovered is almost as good as the best attempts at providing a roof.

Minimum requirements:
- The trees must be at least 6 inches in diameter at the butt end and over 16 feet long

Provide proof of the following as pictures or video (<2 mins):
- Your 2 trees before they are peeled
- Your 2 trees after they are peeled and up off the ground

☐ Drop a 6 inch to 8 inch dead standing tree with a bow saw
☐ Drop a 6 inch to 8 inch dead standing tree with a chainsaw
☐ Drop a 6 inch to 8 inch live tree with a bow saw
☐ Drop a 6 inch to 8 inch live tree with a chainsaw
☐ Limb 4 trees
☐ Peel 2 live trees and put up off the ground to dry
☐ Split and stack dead standing wood as firewood

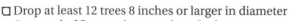

   ☐ Prep 10 junkpoles
      ☐ Cleave 6 shakes with a froe
      Choose 1:
         ☐ Build 12 feet of junkpole fence
         ☐ Repair 24 feet of junkpole fence

☐ Drop at least 12 trees 8 inches or larger in diameter
☐ One cord of firewood: cut and stacked
   properly under a roof
☐ Lumber

Straw badge

   • A dozen 2x4s, 1x4s and ⅜x4s
   ☐ Twig construction
      • Five foot tall tomato cage and eight foot tall pole bean trellis
      ☐ 36 feet of junkpole fence plus one mediocre gate with a mediocre latch
      ☐ Plant the tree seeds for 100 feet of living fence – show that 30% have sprouted
         ☐ Plant black locust tree seeds
         ☐ Plant 100 cleavers – show that 20 have sprouted
      ☐ Plant 100 nettles – show that 20 have sprouted
☐ Plant 20 willows – show that 10 have grown
☐ Inoculate two four foot logs with mushroom spawn and
   harvest at least a half pound of mushrooms
☐ Cleave 40 shakes with a froe

☐ Put up three cords of firewood
☐ More lumber

 Wood badge

   • 8 dozen 2x4s, 1x4s and ⅜x4s
☐ Build six rock jacks out of split logs
☐ 120 feet of junkpole fence with one good gate and a good latch
☐ Plant 300 black locust seeds with 50% germination
☐ Plant 300 cleavers with 50% germination
☐ Plant 300 nettles with 50% germination
☐ Plant 60 willows with 50% growth
☐ Plant 40 sweet sap silver maples
☐ Plant 10 cedar trees
☐ Twig construction
   • Six five foot tall tomato cages and three
     eight foot tall pole bean trellises
☐ Plant the tree seeds for 800 feet of living fence
☐ Lay 50 feet of living fence (otherwise known as a hedge)

- [ ] Berm shed
  - 8x8x8 foot with a 5 foot eave
- [ ] Gin pole
  - Lift a 10 foot long, 12 inch diameter log 15 feet off the ground and place it on a structure
- [ ] Outdoor mushrooms
  - Produce at least one pound each of oyster and shiitake mushrooms
- [ ] Indoor mushrooms
  - Produce at least one pound each of enokitake, oyster and shiitake mushrooms
- [ ] Enhance garden beds with mycelium
- [ ] Skiddable firewood shed
- [ ] Cleave 200 shakes with a froe

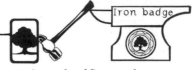

Iron badge

- [ ] Put up six cords of firewood
- [ ] Even more lumber
  - Two hundred 2x4s, 1x4s and ⅜x4s
- [ ] Build 24 rock jacks out of split logs
- [ ] Plant the tree seeds for 2000 feet of living fence
- [ ] "Lay the hedge" for 200 feet of living fence
- [ ] Humus well
- [ ] Junkpole fence around one acre (total of at least 836 feet) with four good gates and good latches
- [ ] Plant the seeds to restore a creek bed from a dry gully
  - 100 feet wide and 800 feet long
- [ ] Berm shed
  - 3 cells with 5 foot eaves, each cell is 12x12x12 foot
- [ ] Build two skiddable structures
- [ ] Bigger gin pole
  - Lift a 16 foot long, 15 inch diameter log 16 feet off the ground and place it on a structure
- [ ] Produce at least ten pounds each of oyster and shiitake mushrooms

---

Sample Sand Badge BB: Drop a 6 to 8 inch dead standing tree with a bow saw

This project will be dropping a 6 to 8 inch dead standing tree with hand tools (bow saw, cross cut saw, axe, etc.). Larger trees are fine if it makes sense for your woodland plans.

Harvested dead trees are a great material for log structures, log furniture, firewood, hugelkultur and hundreds of other projects!

Dead trees are usually less structurally sound than live trees, so use extra caution.

Provide proof of the following as pictures or video (<2 mins):
- Your chosen tree to cut
- Action shot about half way through felling the tree showing your notch/ wedge cut completed
- Fallen tree
- Measurement across the stump showing the diameter

Sample Sand Badge BB: Split and stack dead standing wood for firewood

This project will be to split and stack dead standing wood as firewood.

You will need to stack at least one half of a face cord; this means 4 feet long by 4 feet tall for the length of the firewood you are cutting.

All of the wood must be about 15.5 inches long. Nothing is allowed to be shorter than 15 inches and nothing longer than 16 inches.

Provide proof of the following as pictures or video (<2 mins):
- Your dead standing wood you are starting with
- The wood cut
- Starting the stack (and it is clear that the wood is all about 15 to 16 inches long)
- The stack about 2/3 done (still clear that all of the wood is all about 15 to 16 inches long)
- The completed stack (still clear that all of the wood is all about 15 to 16 inches long)

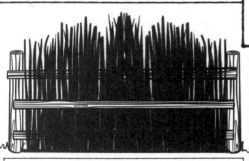

Sample Sand Badge BB: Build 12 feet of junkpole fence

Otis is impressed that you built a strong fence using materials that other people burn in an attempt at "wildfire fuel reduction."

Provide proof of the following as pictures or video (<2 mins):
- Area without a fence
- Fence under construction
- Completed fence
- Show details of every type of joint

Minimum requirements:
- Deer proof (eight feet high)
- Will hold chickens in (no gaps that a layer hen could get through)
- Joinery that will last at least seven years

Clarifications:
- Building a fence section as short as 10.5 feet will still count for this BB
- This BB assumes that the posts or rock jacks are already in place
- Harvesting junkpoles is a different BB

Long-Term Carbon Sink

"Biochar (charcoal) from wildfires can help soil hold more water, nutrients, and soil life for 1000 years! You can do this yourself, no wildfires needed."

Greg Martin, biochar.com

Chapter 16

Round Wood Woodworking

It would be more accurate to call this aspect "Round Wood and Green Wood Woodworking" but that title would be too long.

Round wood is a joy and a challenge to work with. It provides much more strength than dimensional lumber but has bends and curves to work with. Notches, joints and connections become more interesting.

Fresh green wood will shrink, which can be a useful property. Green wood is also much easier to carve than dry wood.

This aspect allows you to show that you've mastered both round wood and green wood woodworking skills. The badge requires zero glue and rarely any metal. Everything is built from raw logs, branches and sticks. Nothing starts with dimensional lumber or prepared blanks.

Power tools can be okay, but, in general, let's use fewer power tools. Some projects specify no power tools.

Featured Sand Badge BB: Three log bench

The three log bench is a bench with two logs as the legs of the bench, and the third log is used for sitting on.

For this BB, you must create two saddle joints. This means cutting a curved shape into the legs to hold the bench log, OR cutting curved shapes into the bench log to sit on the legs.

Minimum requirements:

- Saddle notches to join the seat and base logs (saddles can be on the base logs or the seat log)
- 7 feet minimum overall length for the bench
- 16-18 inches height to the seat top
- Seat log needs to be at least 11 inches in diameter
- Hewn seat surface needs to be at least 6 inches wide
- Hewn top
- Peeled logs

Provide proof of the following as pictures or video (<2 mins):

- Your three log chunks that you are starting with
- Your three log chunks shaped
- Final product showing length, height and seating surface width

Clarifications:

- Chainsaws are allowed for this BB but the finished sitting surface must be smoothed/hewn with a hand tool

Sand badge

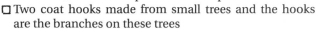

☐ Club style mallet
☐ Compound mallet (smaller dry stick goes into a bigger green stick (head))
☐ Carve a simple first-timer spoon
☐ Two coat hooks made from small trees and the hooks are the branches on these trees
☐ Add one horizontal log to berm/hugelkultur scaffolding
☐ Three log bench
Dry peg in green wood project (build one):
   ☐ 4 coat hooks
   ☐ Half log bench (six feet long) on four legs
   ☐ Saw horse
   ☐ Saw buck
   ☐ Stool

Straw badge

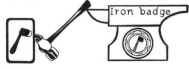

☐ Lightweight stool
☐ Shaving horse
☐ 3 three log benches
☐ Carve a nice, lightweight spoon you can eat with
☐ Bowsaw frame
☐ Decent sawhorse
☐ Decent sawbuck
☐ Basic heavy kitchen chair with a back

☐ Shrink pot
☐ Japanese chisel box made from a block of firewood
☐ Pole lathe
☐ Bowl from a pole lathe
☐ Honey dipper from pole lathe
☐ Lightweight kitchen chair
☐ Heavy table
☐ Skiddable shed for green woodworking
   • Includes a cleaving brake, a place to dry wood/pegs and storage space for shaving horse, pole lathe and other tools
☐ Proenneke hinge – using root wood
☐ Really nice door latch
☐ Light and excellent bowsaw frame

Wood badge

Iron badge

☐ Light dining room table (no metal or glue)
☐ Wood log trough
☐ Magnificent roundwood bed
☐ Two really nice wood bowls
☐ Two really nice wood plates

☐ A steamed wood project
☐ Swinging bench in a skiddable structure
☐ Outdoor firewood rack

- [ ] 2 nice outdoor chairs
- [ ] Rocking chair
- [ ] Bunk beds
- [ ] 2 more lightweight kitchen chairs
- [ ] Carve 2 large spoons for cooking/serving and 3 small spoons for eating
- [ ] Excellent shaving horse
- [ ] Curtain rods
- [ ] Picnic table without dimensional lumber
- [ ] Deck railing
- [ ] Wofati freezer
    - 200 square feet of freezer space and 100 square feet of root cellar space

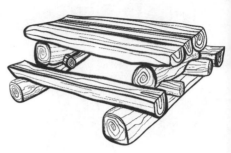

Sample Sand Badge BB: Compound mallet

This mallet is similar to the club style mallet. However, this one is made out of two pieces of wood instead of one.

With this mallet, a dry piece of wood serves as the handle, fitting into the green wood head (freshly cut piece of wood). The idea is that the green wood head will shrink and further tighten itself to the handle.

A hole is made all the way through the head, which the handle is inserted into. This should be a very basic and simply built mallet, able to be built pretty quickly.

Minimum requirements:
- Green (fresh) head
- Dry handle passes all the way through the head
- Big enough to be useful. At least as big and heavy as a common hammer
- No wedge
- Made with hand tools only

Provide proof of the following as pictures or video (<2 mins):
- Your chunks of wood that you are starting with (one is clearly green and the other dry)
- Progress about half way through with the hand tools you have decided to use
- Final product

Sample Sand Badge BB: Green wood stool with dry wood legs

Holes are made in the green wood and the dry leg pieces are inserted into it.

You can either use a thick cross-cut disk of a log or a half a section of a log. You can use 4 legs but 3 will be more stable.

Provide proof of the following a pictures or video (<2 mins):
- Your chunks of wood that you ar starting with
- Progress about half way through with the hand tools you have decided to use for this
- Final product

Minimum requirements:
- Must be at least 16 inches high
- Must be stable on its legs (this is why 3 legs is easier)
    - If using a half a log it must be at least 10 inches diameter (before being halved) and at least 14 inches long
    - If using a disk from a log it must be at least 12 inches in diameter and 5 inches thick

Clarifications:
- "Hand tools" means non-powered tools. No battery/electrically powered drills.
- The log section can be harvested with a chainsaw

46

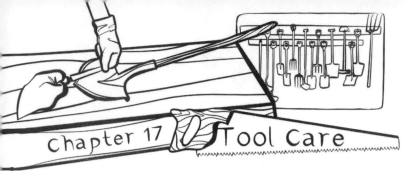

Otis needs to know his tools will be properly cared for. He values his tools more than his house and his truck combined! He has witnessed folks treating their tools poorly – as if you just use them once and throw them away. He is worried about younger folks not having the knowledge for proper tool care. This aspect is to record proof that you know how to take damn good care of tools!

Featured Sand Badge BB: Make a wedge-style handle

Handles occasionally break and need to be replaced. This BB is for the style of handle that will have a wedge driven in to hold the head on the handle.

Examples of tool handles that qualify for this BB are:
- Axe
- Hatchet
- Maul
- Sledge
- Hammer
- Pick
- Pickaxe
- Pulaski

Provide proof of the following as pictures or video (<2 mins):
- Tool with missing/broken/inadequate handle
- New handle under construction
- Tool with new wedge-style handle installed
- Show the wedge installed

- ☐ Sharpen a knife
- ☐ Sharpen a hatchet
- ☐ Sharpen a chainsaw chain
- ☐ Sharpen, clean and oil a shovel
- ☐ Clean the shop
- ☐ Make a wedge-style handle

Bicycle maintenance - complete 2 points from the following:
- ☐ Go to Freecycles and "build" a bicycle to their standards - 2 points
- ☐ Repair a flat tire on the front wheel of a bicycle - ½ point
- ☐ Repair a flat tire on the rear wheel of a bicycle - ½ point
- ☐ Adjust brakes on a bicycle - ½ point
- ☐ Adjust shifters on a bicycle - ½ point
- ☐ Clean and oil chain on a bicycle - ½ point

Sharpen one of the following:
- ☐ Another hatchet
- ☐ Axe
- ☐ Maul
- ☐ Spud
- ☐ Pick, mattock or other tough earthworking tool

Sharpen one of the following:
- ☐ Machete
- ☐ Hori hori knife
- ☐ Drawknife

Sharpen one of the following:
- ☐ Scissors
- ☐ Pruners
- ☐ Loppers

Sharpen one of the following:
- ☐ Bow saw
- ☐ Hand saw
- ☐ Pruning saw
- ☐ Sharpen 3 more knives
- ☐ Sharpen a chisel
- ☐ Sharpen a drill bit
- ☐ Sharpen a scythe
- ☐ Sharpen teeth on a sawmill
- ☐ Make another wedge-style handle
- ☐ Make a pin-style handle

Straw badge

- ☐ Thorough chainsaw sharpening
- ☐ Clean and oil a stationary power tool
- ☐ Clean and oil a portable power tool
- ☐ Remove rust, clean and oil a hand tool
- ☐ Optimize space in the shop
  - Improving storage, shelving, project space, signage, etc
  - At least two and a half days (oddball rules)
- ☐ Change the oil and do full service on a vehicle/tractor
- ☐ Demonstrate use of category 1 to category 2 sleeves
- ☐ Clean, grease and oil a tractor implement

- ☐ Repair a dozen bicycles
- ☐ Make 3 more wedge-style handles
- ☐ Make 3 more pin-style handles
- ☐ Sharpen a dozen twist drill bits
- ☐ Sharpen 6 spade drill bits
- ☐ Sharpen 2 forstner drill bits

- ☐ Sharpen 2 auger drill bits
- ☐ Sharpen a dozen knives
- ☐ Sharpen a hand planer
- ☐ Sharpen two flat edge chisels
- ☐ Sharpen four gouges
- ☐ Sharpen two dozen hand tools
  - Including at least 3 saw blades
- ☐ Sharpen four serrated knife blades
- ☐ Sharpen a band saw blade
- ☐ Sharpen a scythe 2 additional times
- ☐ Chainsaw: make a video for the public about one chainsaw
  - Presented as a video to care for this make and model of chainsaw

Wood badge

- ☐ Augment an existing roof to create more storage space
- ☐ Build a small, portable tool shed
  - On skids or wheels, lockable, at least 6 feet by 10 feet and 7 feet high inside with a workbench
- ☐ Optimize space in the shop (or tool shed)
  - At least 7 days (oddball rules)
- ☐ Do touch up paint on a vehicle or piece of outdoor equipment
- ☐ Build a garden tool cleaning station
- ☐ Add natural light to a dark workspace
- ☐ Create a materials storage shed on skids
  - At least 100 square feet of storage
- ☐ Create a dry place to park a piece of equipment (tractor/truck/UTV/etc.)

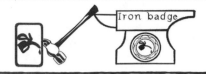

Iron badge

No Iron badge at this time

Minimum requirements:
- The edge is free of nicks and looks sharp when done

Provide proof of the following as pictures or video (<2 mins):
- Closeup of the dull edge
- Action shot of sharpening
- Closeup of sharp edge

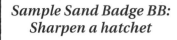

Sample Sand Badge BB: Sharpen a hatchet

You can use a sharpening puck, file, sharpening stone, angle grinder, bench grinder, rock or any other method you think will work.

Sample Straw Badge BB: Sharpen a scythe

To get certified for this BB, post:
- Explanation of your scythe type and how you are going to sharpen it
- Video of dull blade trying to cut grass clearly showing it's not sharp, or close up clearly showing dull edge
- The sharpening process (perhaps peening, perhaps grinding, perhaps using a stone, etc)
- Video of sharp blade easily cutting grass, or close up clearly showing sharp edge

This BB applies to European, American or any other stand-up cutting scythe. The techniques may vary between the types of scythes so do some research and take the steps that are appropriate for your tool.

Sample Straw Badge BB: Make a video of sharpening a chainsaw

To get certified for this BB, post a 2-minute video that demonstrates the following:
- Show the difference between
  - Quick field sharpening
  - Thorough sharpening (including rakers)

There are many schools of thought in sharpening a chainsaw. Show us yours.

49

Chapter 18

Earthworks

This aspect is about modifying your landscape to suit our permaculture goals and demonstrating familiarity with large, earth moving equipment. High on the list is physical access around the site, creating texture and developing ponds without liners.

Make a hole in the ground that is 2 feet in diameter and at least a foot deep.
- Pour in 5 gallons of water and prove that the water is gone in less than 60 minutes
- Compact the soil (probably with different kinds of digging bars, or a piece of rebar stabbed into the hole a hundred times)
- Repeat the 5 gallon test with water remaining for at least an hour

Provide proof of the following as pictures or video (<2 mins):
- Show the new hole
- Show how long it took to drain 5 gallons
- Show the compaction process
- Show the new 5 gallons going in
- Show a toothpick marking the water line once the water is in
- Show that the water level has not dropped more than a half inch in an hour

Featured Sand Badge BB: Seal a tiny pond

We are going to add a tiny bit of edge in your landscape. A very small pond that will probably fill up with "stuff" and disappear in a few years – but that little bit of diversity will remain for decades.

You will build and seal a very small pond. Very, very small. Stupid small. But easy! Very, very easy. And small. And sealed!

There are several ways to make a pond hold water. For this BB, we will emulate a pig wallowing and its hooves compacting.

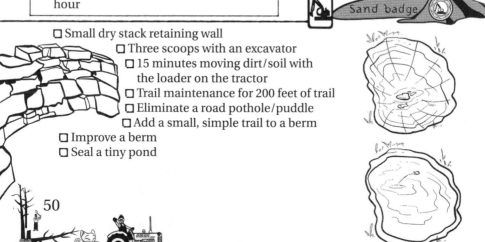

Sand badge

- ☐ Small dry stack retaining wall
- ☐ Three scoops with an excavator
- ☐ 15 minutes moving dirt/soil with the loader on the tractor
- ☐ Trail maintenance for 200 feet of trail
- ☐ Eliminate a road pothole/puddle
- ☐ Add a small, simple trail to a berm
- ☐ Improve a berm
- ☐ Seal a tiny pond

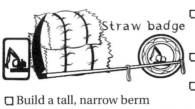

□ Make 100 feet of proper road
  • Must have a crown or other form of drainage and side ditches where appropriate
□ Dry stack retaining wall
  • At least 4 feet tall and 6 feet long
□ Five loads with a dump trailer

□ Build a tall, narrow berm
  • At least 15 feet tall and 20 feet long, 9 feet wide or less
□ Build a small, shallow pond that holds water without a liner
  • About 20 feet in diameter, 4 feet deep with proper dam and spillway
□ Trail maintenance for 1000 feet of trail
□ Add simple trails to berms
□ Add a 50 foot trail to relatively flat rocky ground
□ Add a 50 foot trail to steep, rocky ground
□ 100 feet of road maintenance
  • Eliminating potholes, ruts and washboards, restoring crown and improving ditches and drain points

PEP

Earthworks

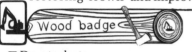

□ Dry stack steps
  • At least 5 steps that are 2 feet wide
□ Dry stack retaining walls
  • At least 4 different walls that are at least 48 square feet each
□ Dry stack wall
  • At least 4 feet high and 15 feet long
  • Add a 2 foot moon gate and get a twofer with the community badge
□ Holzer-style terrace
  • At least 120 feet long by 12 feet wide
□ Build a full size pond that holds water without a liner (sealed bowl style)
  • ¼ acre, at least 10 feet deep and the dam is no taller than 8 feet
□ Create a full size berm
  • At least 15 feet tall and 100 feet long and no more than 27 feet wide
  • 6 foot wide paths about halfway up on each side
□ Parking lot
  • Facilitate parking for at least 3 big pickup trucks with room to turn around
□ Create 3 tent pads
□ Ditches to move water
  • Sealed without a liner and at least 200 feet
□ Earthworks for preparing to build a structure
□ Make 600 feet of proper road
□ Add a 100 foot trail to relatively flat rocky ground
□ Add a 100 foot trail to steep, rocky ground
□ 600 feet of road maintenance

- ☐ Dry stack sun scoop
  - 7 feet tall and 10 foot diameter
- ☐ A Holzer spring terrace
- ☐ Another 200 feet of ditches to move water
- ☐ Build a second full size pond (sealed bowl style)
- ☐ Dry stack steps
  - At least 10 steps that are at least 4 feet wide
- ☐ Season extender rocket mass heater
  - At least 8 feet tall and 30 feet long with a stratification chamber
    - ☐ Earthworks for preparing to build a second structure
    - ☐ 3 passive garden heaters
      - 20 foot deep 6 inch hole in the ground with steel casing
      - 4 foot tall cap with glass on south side
      - Black ¾ inch tube exposed to glass and reaching bottom of hole
  - ☐ Garden ATI
    - Reflecting pond (at least 400 square feet)
    - Double winter heat capture using wofati techniques
    - Flat wall, 7 feet tall, 15 feet wide
- ☐ Large natural swimming pool with a level spot next to it
  - Swimming area is at least 400 square feet and 8 feet deep
  - Water cleaning area is at least 400 square feet, fully planted
- ☐ Build a full size pond that is based on a dam reaching bedrock, rather than a sealed bowl

A dry stack wall is simply stacked rocks that form a wall without using mortar or other types of cement.

Sample Sand Badge BB: Small dry stack retaining wall

Minimum requirements:
- Your wall should be at least 2 feet tall and 4 feet long
- Primarily built using 2 rocks over 1 and 1 rock over 2 technique
- Gravel foundation with good drainage to prevent puddling of icy water
- Wall is much thicker at the bottom than at the top
  - This will give the wall the appearance, in the end, that it is leaning into the dirt
- There is a sharp gravel fill between the wall and dirt
  - Not rounded gravel or sand
  - The gravel is compacted and some of the rocks might rest on some of the gravel

Provide proof of the following as pictures or video (<2 mins):
- Your area before starting
- Your gravel foundation with drainage
- Progress about halfway through, showing some of the rocks stacked and with the gravel behind the wall
- Finished project showing the size of the wall

Sample Sand Badge BB: *Fix road pothole/puddle*

Mud puddles always grow into potholes. Potholes will always grow into an impassable road. Prove to Otis that you are not shy about good road maintenance.

There are many schools of thought on how to best repair a puddle or pothole. Rather than having a different BB for each technique, show us the technique you used for your pothole/puddle.

Provide proof of the following as pictures or video (<2 mins):
- The pothole/puddle in the road that is to be eliminated
- The repair underway
- The road without the pothole or puddle anymore

Sample Straw Badge BB: *Build a small pond without a liner*

There are many ways to build a pond. What is best is going to depend on where it is built, what the subsoil is like and what equipment you have access to.

Provide proof of the following as pictures or video (<2 mins):
- The site before the pond
- The dam under construction
- The spillway under construction
- The disturbed soil being seeded
- The final product filling with water
- Pond full of water

Minimum requirements:
- Creation of a small pond that holds water without a liner
- About 300 square feet in surface area
- At least 4 feet deep
- Importing clay is discouraged, but allowed

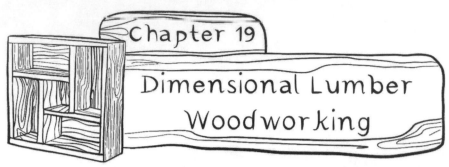

Chapter 19

Dimensional Lumber Woodworking

These projects involve dimensional lumber, either from a sawmill or purchased. This aspect involves construction, cabinetry, and fine woodworking. Plywood, waferboard, or particleboard are not permitted.

Power tools, nails, and screws are used, but hopefully less than in most construction. We'd like to see a little more emphasis on good joinery and much less glue.

No paint. Possibly some tung oil or linseed oil - but just a little. A deliberate emphasis on untreated wood.

Minimum requirements:
- At least 5 inches tall by 18 inches wide
  - Some means of hanging or posting the sign
- No treated wood
- Lettering and images are burned
- Must finish with tung oil or linseed oil (or else the burned image disappears)

Featured Sand Badge BB:
Wood burned sign

Provide proof of the following as pictures or video (<2 mins):
- The wood and your burning tools
- The sign getting burned
- The sign getting oiled
- The sign hanging or posted

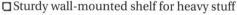

☐ Wood-burned sign

Swanson list - complete 2:
☐ Simple beginner bird house
☐ Lay 10 sticks for decking
☐ Sturdy firewood rack
☐ Two step stool
☐ Sturdy wall-mounted shelf for heavy stuff
  - At least 6 feet long, 18 inches deep and can hold 500 lbs of stuff
☐ Wood box/crate
☐ Install 40 square feet of boards to a structure for siding (inside or out)
☐ Simple, open toolbox

Sand badge

Straw badge

4 additional items from the Swanson list
☐ Basic shelves
  - Custom sized for a need, at least 2 shelves high and 6 feet wide
☐ Bench with a back
☐ Small deck
☐ Picnic table

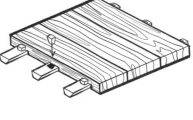

□ Knockdown shelves
  • Zero glue or metal, 3 shelves tall and 2-6 feet wide
      □ Cutting board
          • Zero glue or metal, 2 dovetail splines and pegs
          • Inch and a half thick and at least 12 inches by 18 inches
      □ Adirondack chair
      □ Rolly shelf
          • At least 7 feet tall, 30 inches deep and 75 inches wide
      □ Mediocre folding chair
      □ Good folding chair
      □ Simple bed or bunk bed
      □ Wood bucket (almost watertight)
          • Uses no glue, holds 3 gallons and has a handle
      □ Chest of drawers
          • At least 3 drawers and each drawer is at least 12 inches deep, 18 inches wide and 6 inches tall
      □ Clever picnic table
          • Featuring some type of transformation

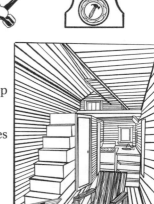

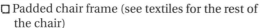

□ Fine floor
□ Padded chair frame (see textiles for the rest of the chair)
□ Couch frame (see textiles for the rest of the couch)
□ Wood bucket (watertight)
□ Storage chest
  • Lid hinge is a wooden knuckle joint
  • At least 24 inches wide, 14 inches high and 20 inches deep
  • No metal or glue
□ Blanket chest
  • Padded seat and at least 36 inches wide, at least 20 inches high and 16 inches deep
  • No metal or glue
□ Japanese nested tool box with a hinged lid
  • Hinge is a wooden knuckle joint
  • At least 24 inches wide, 14 inches high and 10 inches deep
  • No metal or glue
□ Japanese tool chest
  • Two drawers and one swinging door

Skiddable structure (pick two)
□ Sauna
  • Interior at least 5x10 and 7 feet tall with seating for 12 and a rocket heater
□ Hammock hut
  • Interior at least 8x16 and 8 feet tall
  • Broad, strong roof (to hold up hammocks and hammock chairs) and a floor

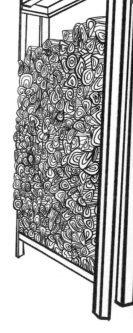

- ☐ Outdoor kitchen
  - Interior at least 6.5x12 and 7 feet tall
  - At least 3 walls
  - Work surface plus shelves with a modular design that allows portable rocket oven and rocket cook tops to be moved in and out
- ☐ Build a skiddable lumber storage shed
  - Interior at least 8x12 and 8 feet tall
- ☐ Build a small, rough porta-cabin on skids
  - Interior dimension of at least 6.5x11 feet
  - Includes a small porch and at least two operable windows
  - Includes an insulated door and simple bunk beds
- ☐ Build a larger, nicer porta-cabin
  - Interior dimension of at least 8x16 feet
  - Includes a porch that can sit two people and at least three operable windows

Final project (pick one)
- ☐ Hot tub hut, complete with a watertight wooden hot tub, on skids
- ☐ A magnificent desk with two hidden compartments
- ☐ A magnificent captain's bed
  - High bed with oodles of drawers underneath and at least two hidden compartments
- ☐ Other projects requiring pre-approval
  - Moving parts
  - Hidden compartments
  - Especially magnificent

Sample Sand Badge BB: Sturdy firewood rack

Minimum requirements:
- Must be able to hold at least one face cord of firewood (32 square feet)
- Requires some structural integrity so a 10 year old won't accidentally tip it over
- Firewood must be exposed to wind, but protected from rain
- No treated wood

Provide proof of the following as pictures or video (<2 mins):
- Location where the rack will go
- Construction partially underway
- The finished rack
- Explanation of how it won't tip over

Sample Sand Badge BB:
Simple open toolbox

Minimum requirements:
- At least 16 inches long
- A carrying handle
- No paint, stain or oil

Provide proof of the following as pictures or video (<2 mins):
- Wood you're starting with
- Construction partially underway
- Finished toolbox

Sample Wood Badge BB:
Wood bucket - almost watertight

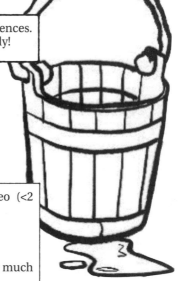

An old technique that is rich in woodworking experiences. Completing this BB will impress Otis… and everybody!

Minimum requirements:
- At least 3 gallons
- No glue
- With handle
- Almost watertight (or better)

Provide proof of the following as pictures or video (<2 mins):
- The wood you're starting with
- Construction partially underway
- The finished bucket filled with water
- The finished bucket 2 minutes later showing how much water has leaked out

Chapter 20
Rocket

Build, operate and maintain wood burning contraptions that cut energy and wood use by 90% while providing luxurious comfortable heat. Including rocket mass heaters, rocket ovens, rocket cooktops, rocket water heaters, outdoor kitchens and so on...

**Featured Sand Badge BB:
Build a Dakota fire hole
and cook some food**

Provide proof of the following as pictures or video (<2 mins):
- Fire starting materials with cold Dakota fire hole
- Building the Dakota fire hole
- Starting materials before fire with cold Dakota fire hole
- Fire started
- Additional wood added
- Food cooking
  - If using a pan or pot, show it resting on something to keep from plugging the exhaust of the system

 Sand badge

☐ Start and operate a J-tube rocket mass heater for 1 hour
☐ Start and operate a batch box rocket mass heater for 1 hour
☐ Start a rocket oven and bake something
☐ Start a rocket cooktop and cook something
☐ Start a rocket water heater and get the water temperature over 140 degrees Fahrenheit
☐ Use a rocket J-tube to boil a gallon of water
☐ Do the annual ash cleanout of a rocket mass heater
☐ Spread some ash on a garden spot (just a dusting)
☐ Build a Dakota fire hole and cook some food

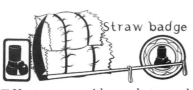

Straw badge

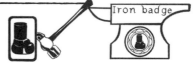

☐ Heat a space with a rocket mass heater
  for one week
☐ Build a J-tube style rocket mass heater

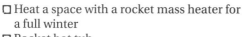

Wood badge

PEP

Rocket

☐ Heat a space with a rocket mass heater for one month
☐ Build an 8 inch J-tube rocket "engine"
  • Could be a twofer in metalworking
  • With a grate it could be a J-tube rocket stove
  • Could later be installed into a future (BB) project
☐ Build a second J-tube style rocket mass heater
☐ Build a J-tube style rocket oven
☐ Build a J-tube style unpressurized rocket water heater
☐ Build a J-tube style rocket cook top
☐ Build a J-tube style season extender in a hugelkultur

☐ Heat a space with a rocket mass heater for
  a full winter
☐ Rocket hot tub
☐ Rocket sauna
☐ Shop style rocket heater

Iron badge

    ☐ Rocket forge
    ☐ Rocket glass recycler
      ☐ Outdoor rocket cooker, smoker
        ☐ Ring-of-fire alternative to a campfire
          ☐ Outdoor classroom with butt warmer
          ☐ Experiments in heating a shop very, very fast
          ☐ Experiments in heating a home
            with extremely little wood
        ☐ Outdoor kitchen or outdoor canning kitchen

Sample Sand Badge BB:
Start and operate a J-tube rocket mass heater

Provide proof of the following as pictures or video (<2 mins): • Fire starting materials • Fire started • Additional wood added • More additional wood added	This BB requires you to start and operate a J-tube rocket mass heater for one hour. You are not required to build your own rocket mass heater but you will need access to one.

Sample Sand Badge BB:
Start a rocket oven and bake something

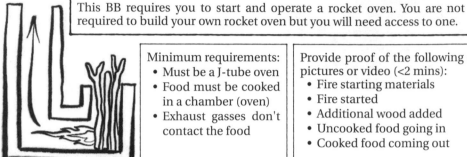

This BB requires you to start and operate a rocket oven. You are not required to build your own rocket oven but you will need access to one.

Minimum requirements:
- Must be a J-tube oven
- Food must be cooked in a chamber (oven)
- Exhaust gasses don't contact the food

Provide proof of the following as pictures or video (<2 mins):
- Fire starting materials
- Fire started
- Additional wood added
- Uncooked food going in
- Cooked food coming out

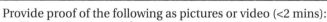

Sample Sand Badge BB:
Start rocket water heater and get to 140F

This BB requires you to start a rocket water heater and get the water temperature over 140 degrees Fahrenheit. You are not required to build your own rocket hot water heater but you will need access to one.

Provide proof of the following as pictures or video (<2 mins):
- Fire starting materials
- Fire started
- Additional wood added
- Water sample being extracted
- Water sample temperature being measured at 140 degrees F or more

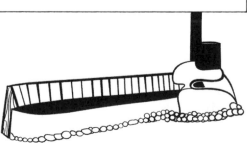

Chapter 21

Food Prep and Preservation

This aspect blends traditional food prep and preservation with modern permaculture tools – covered in a sauce made from gardening, homesteading, foraging and an optional bowl of veganism on the side.

These badges grew into something freakishly massive with a lot of minimum requirements. Eventually, the minimum requirements grew to the point that there was no room left for optional stuff. This is why many amazing food prep and preservation techniques do not appear here.

The following are strictly forbidden:
- Aluminum cookware
- "Non-stick" coatings and similar materials
- Microwave ovens
- Plastic touching the food, including cooking utensils and storage bags

This aspect is not about proving that you are a master chef, but that you can reliably convert a seasonal homestead harvest into a thousand good meals throughout the year.

This is one of those badges where it is very important to remember the difference between "clock time" and "experience time." It might take 30 minutes of clock time for oats to finish cooking, but the amount of time spent actually building experience at cooking oats might be closer to 5 minutes. So for the purposes of this badge, cooking oats counts for 5 minutes.

Featured Sand Badge BB: Cook with a Cast Iron Skillet

A cast iron skillet, when used properly, is just as non-stick as toxic coatings and will last hundreds of years. Prove that you know how to use a cast iron skillet properly.

To show you've completed this Badge Bit, you must provide:
- A ten second long video showing the egg sliding around the pan
- Pics (or video) of the pan cleanup

Minimum requirements:
- You must use a cast iron skillet
- You must cook an egg on the skillet, and it must be able to slide around

Sand badge

Cast iron skillet (select one)
- ☐ Fry an egg so that it slides around
- • Vegan option (do both)
  - ☐ A stack of ten pancakes
  - ☐ Hash browns that fully cover the skillet

Cook at least two cups of grain (or pseudograin) in four different ways
- ☐ Stovetop
- ☐ Rice cooker, crock pot or instapot
- ☐ Solar oven
- ☐ Rocket stove and haybox cooker

Canning (select one)
- ☐ Water bath canning
- ☐ Steam canning

- ☐ Dry food in a solar food dehydrator
- ☐ Vinegar brine pickle something
- ☐ Salt brine ferment/pickle something
- ☐ Cook stir fry
- ☐ Make soup/stew/chowder
- ☐ Make pizza
- ☐ Bake 2 loaves of bread

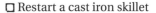 
Straw badge

- ☐ Restart a cast iron skillet

Food Preparation
- ☐ Make 6 quarts of stock from veggie scraps
- ☐ Cook and serve a pound of sunchokes
- ☐ Soup – make 4 types of soup
  - • At least 1 is cooked on a rocket stove or Dakota fire hole and at least 2 are finished in a haybox cooker
- ☐ Bake six things
  - • At least 2 things are baked in a rocket oven and 2 are baked in cast iron
- ☐ Roast 4 pans of food
  - • At least 1 is done in a rocket oven and 1 in cast iron
- ☐ Fry 12 different things
  - • At least 3 things are fried on a rocket stove or Dakota fire hole and 6 are in cast iron
- ☐ Open fire – cook 4 different things
  - • At least 1 item is buried in coals and another is cooked on a spit
- ☐ Make 2 dairy foods (true dairy or vegan):
  - • Hard cheese (counts as two), butter, powdered milk, yogurt, cream, cottage cheese, ice cream, soft cheeses, kefir, or nut milk
- ☐ Make 2 condiments or salad dressings
- ☐ Make 2 kinds of gravy
- ☐ Grind 2 different grains into flour
- ☐ Oils and Fats – press or render a quart of oil or fat

Food Preservation
☐ Pressure can 2 different things
☐ Water bath can 3 different types of food
☐ Storing food in a living state (possibly in a root cellar)
  • At least 20 pounds of each food and at least 6 different species
☐ Dry 6 different types of things
☐ Ferment 4 different types of things
  • At least 1 gallon per type of fermented food
☐ Process grain for storage

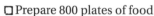

Wood badge

98% of the food for this badge is "organic or better"

75% of the food comes from homesteading, preferably from your own homestead
  • Nearby homestead or wild harvest (forage/hunting/fishing) is ok
    - Their food values need to be "organic or better"
    - Acquired with muscle power (bike/horse/foot/dogsled)
    - Trade, purchase or gifted is fine
☐ Preserve 1 million calories
  • No more than 10% can be one type of thing (i.e. not 500 quarts of canned peaches)
    - 10% bacon, 10% ham, 10% canned pork, is ok
  • Must be at least 24 different types of food
  • No more than 10% can be frozen

☐ Prepare 800 plates of food
  • "Plate" means a meal averaging 500 calories

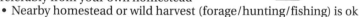

Iron badge

99% of the food for this badge is "organic or better"

90% of the food comes from homesteading, preferably from your own homestead
  • Nearby homestead or wild harvest (forage/hunting/fishing) is ok
    - Their food values need to be "organic or better"
    - Acquired with muscle power (bike/horse/foot)
    - Trade, purchase or gifted is fine
☐ Preserve 4 million calories
  • Must be at least 48 different types of food
☐ Prepare 3200 plates of food
  • At least 400 plates need to be 100% from your homestead
    - Salt from off-site is allowed

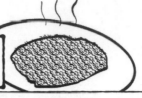

Sample Sand Badge BB:
Fry hash browns

This is one of the vegan alternatives to the "Fry an egg" BB. Show Otis you have experience cooking with pans that aren't coated with toxic gick.

Minimum requirements:
- Use a cast iron skillet
- The hash browns must cover the entire skillet
- The hash browns must make one large intact gob
  - A bit like you are making a giant potato chip from a bunch of grated potatoes
  - Without sticking

To show you've completed this BB, you must provide:
- A video that is no longer than 30 seconds long showing
  - Grated potatoes going in
  - The first flip as one piece, and there is no sticking
  - The single piece being moved onto a plate – no sticking
  - Cleanup
  - Feel free to edit the video and even speed up the video

Sample Sand Badge BB:
Cook grain with a rocket stove and haybox cooker

Minimum requirements:
- Produce at least two cups of grain
- Bring the water and grain to a boil on a rocket stove
  - A Dakota fire pit is acceptable
- Complete the cooking in a haybox cooker
- Haybox cooker can be homemade or an insulated container that uses haybox cooker principles

This is one of the more challenging BBs in the Sand badge of Food Prep. You need to have access to these devices or build simple versions. A rocket stove is not a rocket mass heater. You can build one with a few dozen red clay bricks. Heat the water up to boiling but don't continue to cook past that point. Move the container into a haybox cooker. You can build an official haybox cooker or it can be as simple as a large picnic cooler filled with blankets/towels.

The purpose of this BB is to show that you can cook grain with a very small amount of wood and have experience with insulated slow cooking.

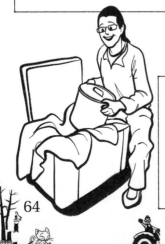

Provide proof of the following as pictures or video (<2 mins):
- The grain and water boiling on a rocket stove
- Your heated uncooked grain being transferred to a haybox cooker (with some sort of watch or timer)
  - Must show how the grain isn't cooked yet
- Your cooked grain coming out of a haybox cooker (with some sort of watch or timer)
- Show the final product is at least two cups of grain

Sample Sand Badge BB:
Dehydrate food in a solar dehydrator

Minimum requirements:
- Use a solar food dehydrator
  - A proper solar food dehydrator is preferred, but we will accept the use of the "sunny rocks technique" or even "the sunny windshield technique"
- You must have two pounds of food before dehydration

Provide proof of the following as pictures or video (<2 mins):
- Food on a scale before dehydration (or, obviously far more than two pounds)
- Food in your solar dehydrator before dehydration (with entire structure of dehydrator)
- Food in your solar dehydrator after dehydration (with entire structure of dehydrator)

Sample Sand Badge BB:
Make two loaves
of bread

Any kind of bread is acceptable. The two loaves can be "normal," paleo, vegan, gluten free, a "quick bread" like banana bread, or Paul's "polydough."

Minimum requirements:
- Two loaves of bread
- The bread must be slice-able and not crumble to pieces
- It shouldn't be burnt
- Not using a bread machine
- The two loaves can be the same or different (cinnamon raisin, jalapeno, herb, etc.)
- Can be combined with the rocket oven BB in the Rocket Sand badge for a twofer

Provide proof of the following as pictures or video (<2 mins):
- Link to or post the recipe you used
- The ingredients getting mixed
- The completed loaves and a slice of each of them
  - Showing the loaves are not burnt, are fully cooked, and slice well

65

Chapter 22

Animal Care

Animals are a benefit to any homestead no matter what you eat.

Extra care was expended on developing the sand and straw badges so that they can be completed by a vegan. A great deal of this was accomplished by creating a nurturing environment for beneficial wild animals and insects.

The wood and iron badges are an effort to move to a much higher level of animal care than is found on most homesteads.

Featured Sand Badge BB: Create frog habitat

Minimum requirements:
- Spring, summer and fall water with mud
- Lots of stout plants near the water to protect the frogs from predators
- Lots of insect attracting plants
- Hiding places in the water for frogs/tadpoles to hide from predators
- At least 20 square feet of water surface
- No pond liner (hint: there's a BB in Earthworks for sealing a pond)

Provide proof of the following as pictures or video (<2 mins):
- Where frog habitat will be built and your materials
- Progress of building the frog habitat
- Completed frog habitat that obviously meets the minimum requirements

Sand badge

Complete five:
- ☐ Build a nice birdhouse for a specific species of bird
- ☐ Build a mason bee house (possibly other solitary bees)
- ☐ Perform maintenance on a mason bee house (possibly other solitary bees)
- ☐ Make a bee/insect watering station
- ☐ Move a yellowjacket nest from where it is a bother to where it is a value
- ☐ Catch a honey bee swarm with a bait hive/swarm trap
- ☐ Rescue a honey bee swarm
- ☐ Plant a three season nectar harvest for pollinators
- ☐ Build a ladybug house

- ☐ Build a bat house
- ☐ Build an insect hotel
- ☐ Scythe and bale 1 bale of hay
- ☐ Scythe and bale 1 bale of straw
- ☐ Create a brush pile near a garden for animal/insect diversity habitat
- ☐ Create 6 different toad habitats
  - ☐ Plant 60 mulberry tree seeds
  - ☐ Create snake/lizard habitat
  - ☐ Create a live rodent trap
    - ☐ Create at least a pint of Holzer bone sauce
    - ☐ Share appropriate kitchen scraps
- ☐ Milk a cow or goat or sheep - 1 gallon for cows, 1 quart for others
- ☐ Plant seeds for hummingbirds
- ☐ Putting out some winter straw to help the animals stay warm
  - ☐ Fecal parasite test
  - ☐ Sheep health check
  - ☐ Training animals for goodies
  - ☐ Cleaning a shelter
  - ☐ Cleaning out at least 4 nesting boxes for chickens

- ☐ Grow sprouts as a winter feed for fowl
- ☐ Remove algae from a trout pond
- ☐ Add aeration strategy to a trout pond
- ☐ Stock a trout pond with trout
- ☐ Move animals to a new paddock
- ☐ Collect 12 eggs from your fowl
- ☐ Food/water/egg/safety check for your fowl
- ☐ Food/water/safety check for your 4 legged livestock
- ☐ Create dragonfly habitat
- ☐ Create frog habitat
- ☐ Manage breeding and support a farm cat resulting in at least 6 kittens
- ☐ Chicken - slaughter and clean
- ☐ Duck - slaughter and clean
- ☐ Turkey - slaughter and clean
- ☐ Guinea fowl - slaughter and clean
- ☐ Quail - slaughter and clean
- ☐ Pigeon - slaughter and clean
- ☐ Rabbit - slaughter and clean
- ☐ Guinea pig - slaughter and clean
- ☐ Goose - slaughter and clean

PEP

Animal Care

Straw badge

35 points required
- Up to 15 new points from Sand badge allowed
  - Each item counts for 1 point

- ☐ Set up a stock tank that won't freeze in the winter without electricity - 4 points
  - Only applies in climates where freezing is a routine issue
- ☐ Set up a moveable electric fence for paddock shift systems (show a move)
  - Using 110v AC power - 1 point
  - Using car battery (kept dry) - 1.5 points
    - ☐ Scythe and bale a dozen bales of hay - 4 points
    - ☐ Scythe and bale a dozen bales of straw - 4 points
    - ☐ Build a manual baler - 3 points
    - ☐ Grow forage for chickens/pigs in a single paddock - 4 points

- ☐ Prove that paddock shift is amazing - 10 points
  - At least 4 paddocks with a 10 foot x10 foot control area that is fenced off
- ☐ Grow a 3 season nectar harvest for pollinators - 10 points
  - At least a dozen species with hundreds of blooms at 2 points in each season (six pics total)
- ☐ Prove that chickens prefer fresh food over organic commercial food - 10 points
  - 2 extra points if the paddock chickens prefer fresh food so much that they eat zero commercial food

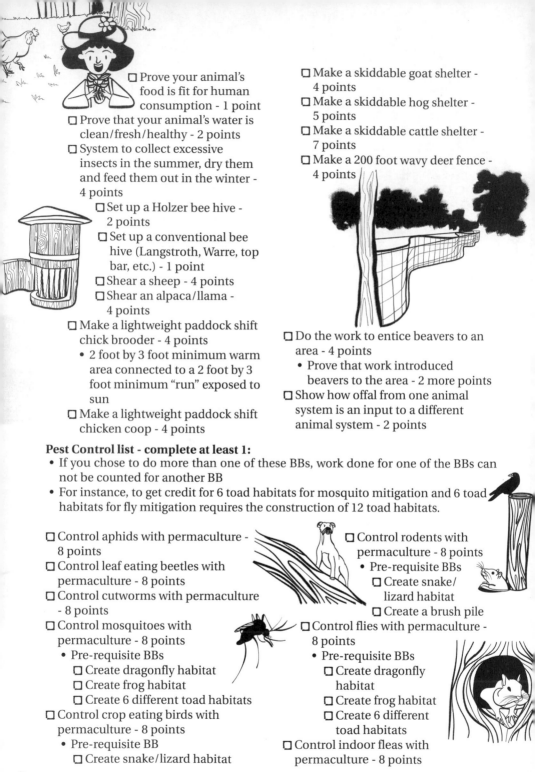

☐ Prove your animal's food is fit for human consumption - 1 point
☐ Prove that your animal's water is clean/fresh/healthy - 2 points
☐ System to collect excessive insects in the summer, dry them and feed them out in the winter - 4 points
    ☐ Set up a Holzer bee hive - 2 points
    ☐ Set up a conventional bee hive (Langstroth, Warre, top bar, etc.) - 1 point
    ☐ Shear a sheep - 4 points
    ☐ Shear an alpaca/llama - 4 points
☐ Make a lightweight paddock shift chick brooder - 4 points
    • 2 foot by 3 foot minimum warm area connected to a 2 foot by 3 foot minimum "run" exposed to sun
☐ Make a lightweight paddock shift chicken coop - 4 points

☐ Make a skiddable goat shelter - 4 points
☐ Make a skiddable hog shelter - 5 points
☐ Make a skiddable cattle shelter - 7 points
☐ Make a 200 foot wavy deer fence - 4 points

☐ Do the work to entice beavers to an area - 4 points
    • Prove that work introduced beavers to the area - 2 more points
☐ Show how offal from one animal system is an input to a different animal system - 2 points

Pest Control list - complete at least 1:
• If you chose to do more than one of these BBs, work done for one of the BBs can not be counted for another BB
• For instance, to get credit for 6 toad habitats for mosquito mitigation and 6 toad habitats for fly mitigation requires the construction of 12 toad habitats.

☐ Control aphids with permaculture - 8 points
☐ Control leaf eating beetles with permaculture - 8 points
☐ Control cutworms with permaculture - 8 points
☐ Control mosquitoes with permaculture - 8 points
    • Pre-requisite BBs
      ☐ Create dragonfly habitat
      ☐ Create frog habitat
      ☐ Create 6 different toad habitats
☐ Control crop eating birds with permaculture - 8 points
    • Pre-requisite BB
      ☐ Create snake/lizard habitat

☐ Control rodents with permaculture - 8 points
    • Pre-requisite BBs
      ☐ Create snake/lizard habitat
      ☐ Create a brush pile
☐ Control flies with permaculture - 8 points
    • Pre-requisite BBs
      ☐ Create dragonfly habitat
      ☐ Create frog habitat
      ☐ Create 6 different toad habitats
☐ Control indoor fleas with permaculture - 8 points

Breeding List:

- Breed a broody hen to hatch at least six chicks - 4 points
- Breed a broody duck to hatch at least six ducklings - 4 points
- Breed a broody turkey to hatch at least four poults- 4 points
- Breed a guinea fowl to hatch at least six keets - 4 points
- Breed a quail to hatch at least six chicks - 4 points
- Breed a pigeon to hatch at least four squabs - 4 points
- Breed a goose to hatch at least six goslings- 4 points
- Breed a goat resulting in at least one kid - 4 points
- Breed a rabbit resulting in at least three kits - 4 points
- Breed an ewe resulting in at least one lamb - 4 points
- Breed a cow resulting in at least one calf - 4 points
- Breed a sow resulting in at least six piglets - 4 points

- Breed a guinea pig resulting in at least six pups - 4 points
- Breed a llama resulting in at least one cria - 4 points
- Breed an alpaca resulting in at least one cria - 4 points
- Breed a working farm dog resulting in at least six puppies - 4 points
- Raising mealworms - 3 points
  - End up with two pounds more mealworms than when you started
- Raising crayfish - 3 points
  - End up with two pounds more crayfish than when you started
- Raising worms - 4 points
  - End up with two pounds more worms than when you started
- Raising black soldier flies - 4 points
  - End up with two pounds more grubs than when you started
- Raising mason bees - 2 points
  - End up with ½ pound of cocoons
- Fish farming - 2 points
  - End up with five pounds more than when you started
  - Prerequisite is to do the stock a trout pond with trout BB

Harvest List:
- Process fish - catch and clean 5 pounds of fish from your pond - 2 points
- Butcher a goat - slaughter and clean - 2 points
- Butcher a sheep - slaughter and clean - 2 points
- Butcher beef - slaughter and clean - 8 points
- Butcher a pig - slaughter and clean - 6 points

Parasite list:
- Prove that your chickens do not have parasites - 4 points
- Prove that your ducks do not have parasites - 4 points
- Prove that your cattle do not have parasites - 4 points

- Prove that your guinea fowl do not have parasites - 4 points

- Prove that your quail do not have parasites - 4 points
- Prove that your pigeons do not have parasites - 4 points
- Prove that your geese do not have parasites - 4 points
- Prove that your llamas do not have parasites - 4 points

- ☐ Prove that your rabbits do not have parasites - 4 points
- ☐ Prove that your alpacas do not have parasites - 4 points
- ☐ Prove that your hogs do not have parasites - 4 points
- ☐ Prove that your cats do not have parasites - 4 points
- ☐ Prove that your dogs do not have parasites - 4 points
- ☐ Prove that your goats do not have parasites - 4 points
- ☐ Prove that your sheep do not have parasites - 4 points
- ☐ Prove that your turkeys do not have parasites - 4 points
- ☐ Prove that your fish do not have parasites - 4 points
- ☐ Prove that your bees do not have parasites - 4 points
- ☐ Prove that your guinea pigs do not have parasites - 4 points

Prerequisites:
- ☐ Prove your animal's food is fit for human consumption
- ☐ Prove that your animal's water is clean/fresh/healthy

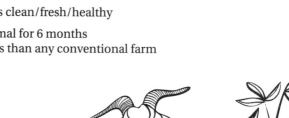

☐ Care for 6 different species of animal for 6 months
- Provide clearly better conditions than any conventional farm
- Primarily skiddable shelters
- No manure handling
- Less than 2% off-property inputs

☐ Harvest 200,000 calories from a domestic animal system
- At least 6 animal products and a minimum of 10,000 calories from each of the 6

60 points required
- Can do up to 30 new points from Sand and Straw lists
☐ Harvest 20 lbs of fiber from a domestic
  animal system - 10 points
☐ Harvest 5 square feet of leather - 8 points
☐ Harvest 5 square feet of fur - 8 points
☐ Seal a 1000 square foot pond with pigs - 12 points
☐ Grow a large three season nectar harvest
  for honeybees - 20 points
  - Minimum of ¼ acre and at least two dozen species
☐ Arrange a hayless system for a ruminant herd - 20 points
☐ Grow forage for chickens/pigs in four paddocks - 10 points
  - At least 12 plant species, obviously more than 20,000 calories of forage per
    paddock

This badge requires you to
care for 12 species of critters.

These six are required:
- Cattle
- Chickens
- Hogs
- Turkey
- Fish
- Honeybees

Six more species required (your choice). Possibilities could be more than what you see on this list:
- Ducks
- Guinea fowl
- Quail
- Pigeons
- Geese
- Guinea pigs for meat
- Working farm dogs
- Working farm cats
- Sheep
- Goats
- Llama
- Alpaca
- Rabbits

General conditions required for all animals for which it applies:
- Primarily skiddable shelters
- No manure handling
- All of the animal systems must be less than 2% off-site input
- Hayless (or dramatic hay reduction system) is required
- Minimal bare dirt under hoof/foot
- Out in green, lush pasture most of the year
- Plenty of shady spots
- Sufficient herd/flock size to satisfy animal's natural needs
- Lack of flies, ticks, etc
- Dry, wind protected shelters
- Cattle butchering offal goes to chickens, pigs, fish, etc., chicken goes to the pigs, dogs, fish, etc
- Little to no predator pressure
- Parasite and disease checks for all species
- Their last day and last 15 minutes are calm and relaxing. Slaughtered on site.

71

❑ Harvest 4 million calories from at least 9 domestic animal systems
- Must include a minimum of:
    - 1 beef animal
    - Dairy (5 lbs butter, 5 lbs cheese, 1 qt cream)
    - 100 eggs
    - 12 butchered chickens
    - 6 turkeys
    - 2 hogs
    - 10 lbs fish
    - 10 lbs honey

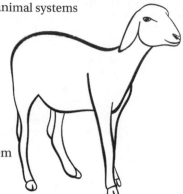

❑ Harvest 80 lbs of fiber from a domestic animal system
❑ Harvest 20 square feet of leather
❑ Harvest 20 square feet of fur

Provide proof that you are breeding and nurturing 12 animal species
- Pampered or treated better than 98% of other domestic animals
- Level 6 animal care is "pampered" and level 7 is "something that would inspire a Disney movie about a little girl and all of her homestead animal friends." Provide some evidence that you might be close to level 7.
- General examples:
    - Come when called
    - Let them "escape" and show you can call/entice them back easily
    - You drink their water
    - You eat their food
    - You've thought deeply about your animal's fears of predation and act accordingly
    - Just because a human would like your "pampering," ensure that your critter would
    - Herbal apothecary in their paddocks
    - Sing or play with you
    - Sleep in their shelter for one night
    - Toys and forms of entertainment for the animals
    - Four seasons of pampering
    - Examples of being people friendly
    - Prolific reproduction
    - Prolific meat/milk production
    - Describe your breeding objectives and plan
    - Describe, for each animal, how your breeding objectives breed out dependence on antibiotics
    - A heated shelter for the 12 coldest days of winter
    - Put out food for them for the 12 coldest days of winter

❑ Prove you are nurturing your cattle
- Minimum of 3 calves from breeding to six months old
- Come willingly to be milked

- ☐ Prove you are nurturing your chickens
  - Chicken breeding program to favor good egg production and foraging on your property
  - Minimum of 100 chickens from hatch to 3 months old under broody hens (no incubators)
- ☐ Prove you are nurturing your hogs
  - Minimum of two dozen hogs from birth to six months old
  - Ensure wallow facilities for the 12 hottest days of the year
- ☐ Prove you are nurturing your turkeys
  - Minimum of a dozen turkeys from under a broody hen to 3 months old
- ☐ Prove you are nurturing your fish
  - 12 or more species of aquatic and riparian plant
  - Variety of water depths, rocks, logs, hiding places
  - No supplemental fish food - sufficient bugs/plants/etc. for them to forage
- ☐ Prove you are nurturing your honeybees
  - Tens of thousands of blooms at 2 points in each season within 150 feet of the hive (about two acres)
  - Includes bear protection, additional winter insulation system, no paint on hive and a bee hut or equivalent system for shade, rain and snow protection
  - Each colony must come from a wild swarm and you must prove that your colony swarmed at least once
  - Each hive is at least 200 feet from any other hive

Prove you are nurturing another species (complete 6)

☐ Breed and nurture ducks	☐ Breed and nurture alpaca
☐ Breed and nurture geese	☐ Breed and nurture guinea pigs
☐ Breed and nurture guinea fowl	☐ Breed and nurture llama
☐ Breed and nurture quail	☐ Breed and nurture working
☐ Breed and nurture pigeons	farm dogs
☐ Breed and nurture rabbits	☐ Breed and nurture working
☐ Breed and nurture goats	farm cats
☐ Breed and nurture sheep	

Sample Sand Badge BB:
Catch a honey bee swarm

If there are colonies of honey bees in your area that are strong and healthy, they will generate a swarm. Collecting that swarm is about a hundred times better than buying a colony of bees that might have poor genetics and be from a region that might be a lot different from your region.

Minimum requirements:
- You must catch a honey bee swarm with a bait hive (swarm trap)

Provide proof of the following as pictures or video (<2 mins):
- An empty bait hive
- The bait hive full of bees

73

Sample Sand Badge BB: Make Holzer bone sauce

It smells a little like an old BBQ grill that needs to be cleaned. By applying it to a tree trunk it will repel deer and other tree nibblers for years. It is an odd process made predominantly of bones.

Minimum requirements:
• You must make at least one pint of Holzer bone sauce

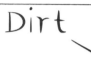

Dirt

Clay

Holzer bone sauce

Provide proof of the following as pictures or video (<2 mins):
• Your setup to make the bone sauce, with bones ready to cook
• The fire
• The fire after it's out
• The setup being opened and pulling out the first spoonful of bone sauce
• Jar holding at least one pint

Sample Sand Badge BB: Clean out 4 chicken nest boxes

Minimum requirements:
• Clean out at least 4 chicken nesting boxes
• Fresh straw or clean wood chips/shavings
• Maybe add a little DE (diatomaceous earth) in the boxes

Provide proof of the following as pictures or video (<2 mins):
• 4 dirty nesting boxes
• Replacing the straw or clean wood chips/shavings
• 4 clean nest boxes

Sample Sand Badge BB: Rabbit - Slaughter and clean

Rabbits are widely considered to be one of the most generous meat returns for grass inputs.

But to harness their great reproductive power for your larder, you must know how to harvest them safely, efficiently, and humanely.

Minimum requirements:
• 1 live rabbit
• Killed in a humane manner
• Processed and either prepared or properly stored within an hour

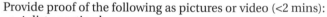

Provide proof of the following as pictures or video (<2 mins):
• Living rabbit
• Rabbit after slaughter, depicting the method used
• Rabbit ready for cooking or freezing/preservation for a later date

chapter 23

Foraging

This badge is about foraging, hunting, trapping, and fishing... with some forage gardening sprinkled in. Must be wild foods – not gleaning or harvesting from an actively cultivated space.

Apples from a neighbor don't count here. Apples from a homestead that has been abandoned for at least five years do count. Apples growing in an odd place where there has never been any cultivation counts too (probably a discarded apple core led to the tree). Apples that are the result of guerilla or forage gardening count too.

Seed balls are a technique for planting stuff without planting it. Just mush the seeds in a ball of compost and clay today and later chuck them into places where you want plants to show up. The compost brings fertility to the process. The clay holds the ball together and helps with germination once there is water present.

Featured Sand Badge BB:
Make 4lbs of
seed balls

PEP

Foraging

Provide proof of the following as pictures or video (<2 mins):
- The seeds in your mixing container
- The balls being created
- The finished balls on a scale showing the weight
- Listing of the seeds you used

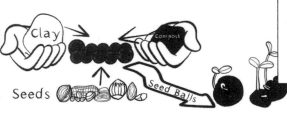

Minimum requirements:
- Make at least 4 lbs (fresh weight) of seed balls
- At least an inch in diameter
- Can either be used immediately or quickly dried for storage (before the seeds germinate)
- At least six different species in each ball
  - At least four of the species are perennials
  - Possible species:
    - Nettle
    - Dandelion
    - Maple
    - Mulberry
    - Apricots
    - Apples
    - Black locust
    - Sepp grain
    - Daikon radish
    - Alfalfa
    - Tomato
    - Sunflower
    - Lupine
    - Squash
    - Kale
    - Turnip
    - Cherry

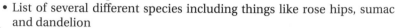

□ Fresh list - harvest one of:
  • Long list of more than 25 different species including things like 1 pound of huckleberries, 2 pounds of elderberries or 20 pounds of plums

□ Dry list - harvest, dry, and store one of the following:
  • List of several different species including things like 1 pound of nettle, 5 pounds of mushrooms or 20 pounds of apples

□ Tea list - make a cup of tea
  • List of several different species including things like rose hips, sumac and dandelion

□ Dish list - prepare a dish (soup, salad, entree, side, etc.) that uses at least a cup of a foraged ingredient
  • List of several different species including things like lambsquarters, burdock root and purslane

□ 4 pounds of seed balls
  • At least an inch in diameter, 6 species and at least 4 species have to be perennials

Sand badge

Complete two of the following:
□ Catch and prepare at least one pound of fish
□ Catch and prepare one wild rabbit or squirrel
□ Harvest maple sap and reduce it down to make 1 pint of syrup
  • Do 2 more items from the Dry list (duplicates are okay)
  • Do 4 more items from the Dish list (duplicates are okay)
  • Do 4 more items from the Fresh list (duplicates are okay)

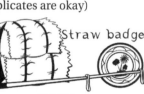

Straw badge

35 points required
  • New items from the Sand Fresh list - ½ point each
  • New items from the Sand Dry list - ½ point each
  • New items from the Sand Tea list - ½ point each
  • New items from the Sand Dish list - ½ point each

□ 20 pounds of seed balls - 4 points
  • Unlimited duplication with different species each time

□ Save seeds from 6 species of wild plants - 2 points
  • Unlimited duplication with different species each time

□ Catch, butcher and preserve at least five pounds of fish or ten pounds of shellfish - 4 points
□ Catch, butcher and preserve five wild rabbits/squirrels - 4 points
□ Catch, butcher and preserve one large mammal (deer, pig, elk, antelope, etc.) - 8 points
□ Catch, butcher and preserve five wild game birds - 4 points
□ Harvest maple sap and reduce it down to make 1 gallon of syrup - 8 points
□ Collect 5 pounds of wild honey (without cutting down tree) - 4 points
□ Guerilla plant 500 woody perennial food seeds or cuttings (not seed balls) - 8 points

PEP

Foraging

Wood badge

☐ Forage 200,000 calories from at least 10 species
  • 6 species of at least 10,000 calories each
    - No more than 4 of the 6 can be animal species
  • At least half of the calories need to be dried for storage that could last more than a year at room temp – possible twofer with Food Prep and Preservation
☐ 10 days eating 90% foraged food
  • 90% by calories, a minimum of 1200 calories per day and at least 6 foraged food types per day
  • Can include preserved foraged foods and they don't need to be consecutive days
☐ 1 mile of trail side forage gardening
  • Grow more than 500 plants near a trail and harvest calories from at least 6 different species

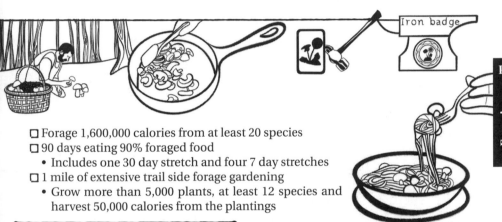

Iron badge

☐ Forage 1,600,000 calories from at least 20 species
☐ 90 days eating 90% foraged food
  • Includes one 30 day stretch and four 7 day stretches
☐ 1 mile of extensive trail side forage gardening
  • Grow more than 5,000 plants, at least 12 species and harvest 50,000 calories from the plantings

---

Sample Sand Badge BB: Catch and prepare a fish

Provide proof of the following as pictures or video (<2 mins):
  • The fish with your fish catching gear and where the fish came from in the background
  • The cleaned/gutted/filleted or otherwise ready-to-cook fish (or on a scale or obviously more than one pound)
  • The prepared dish

Minimum requirements:
  • Catch and prepare at least one pound of fish meat.

Clarifications:
  • This is "Foraging" so the fish can't come from your aquaponics system, nor an aquaculture system, nor a store
  • Multiple small fish or one large fish is allowed

Sample Sand Badge BB: Fresh harvest list

Foraging is like gardening but without all the planting, weeding, nibbler protection or watering. If you live in the country, there are lots of trails and old roads to search. These must be wild foods – not gleaned or harvested from an actively cultivated space.

Plant identification is the most important part of foraging. Get a few good books on the edibles of your region. Be sure you know what you're picking!

Provide proof of the following as pictures or video (<2 mins):
- One of the plants the food came from
- The bounty on a scale showing the weight (or you have so much, there is no need to weigh it)

Clarifications:
- The 1 lb list or the 2 lb list can comprise any combination of the berries listed to add up to the required weight (e.g. one pound of chokecherries and a pound of mulberries satisfies the 2 lb list)

Minimum requirements:
- One pound (total) of:
  - Huckleberries
  - Raspberries
  - Blueberries
  - Aronia
  - Salmonberries
  - True cranberries
  - Serviceberries
  - Blackberries (tiny varieties)
  - Strawberries
- Two pounds of:
  - Blackberries (large varieties)
  - Highbush cranberries
  - Elderberries
  - Grapes
  - Chokecherries
  - Mulberries
  - Sunchokes
  - Asparagus
  - Small cherries (pin, bush, etc.)
- Twenty pounds of:
  - Apples
  - Pears
  - Apricots
  - Plums
  - Hazelnuts
  - Walnuts
  - Chestnuts
  - Hickory nuts
  - Tree cherries (hazelnut shell sized or bigger)

Sample Wood Badge BB: 1 mile of trail side forage gardening

For this BB, you will forage garden 1 mile of trail side! This is a concept Mike and I came up with but I'm sure someone else invented it already. The idea is to plant lots of food crops along a trail. It can be a public or private trail. The idea is that by stewarding the land near that trail it can eventually become a really good place to forage for food.

Provide proof of the following as pictures or video (<2 mins):
- Video of trail when introducing seed balls or planting, and a general idea of what edibles were there to start
- Video of trail for several harvests and showing what plants made it
- Show at least 100 fruit trees at least four inches tall
- Show the weight of food harvested and describe the calories each represents

Minimum requirements:
- 1 mile of trail side forage gardening
- 1 living plant per 10 feet of trail on average (more than 500 plants total)
- Within 20 feet of the trail
- At least six different species
- Can be roadside, for rarely used dirt roads
- The mile can be spread out between multiple stretches of trail
- Harvest 1000 calories each from six different species (can be from existing plants along the mile)
- Harvest at least 10,000 calories total (can go towards the forage 200,000 calorie BB)

Community Living

Bertie's bench
Chapter 24

Thanks to Ashley Lortscher for developing a lot of substance for this aspect.

Community can mean so many things. For the sake of this aspect, "community" is about bringing dozens of productive gardeners onto the same land – possibly under the same roof. Permaculture is largely about replacing petroleum with people. The intent of this aspect is to show Otis how you will be able to attract and retain a community of productive gardeners to help his land thrive for decades to come.

Note that the BBs in this aspect are brutally focused on the tasks that could help BUILD the very exact flavor of community we are seeking. We have winnowed out the hundreds of suggested BBs that were about experiencing community or building other types of community.

Brand a physical location with a sign, as well as make a public thread about it on Permies.com

Featured Sand Badge BB:
Brand a physical location

Berm Shed

Examples of locations to brand:
- Tree
- Structure
- Trail
- Point
- Berm
- Hugelkultur bed
- Pond
- Road
- Freaky big rock
- Cliff
- Gate
- Paddock
- Bench
- Winter sledding spot

Minimum requirements:
- A public thread at Permies.com with pics and some description and story
- A sign at the location
  - A small bit of art, story or significance

For ideas on how to make a sign, check out Dimensional Lumber's BB on Making a Sign.

To document your completion of the BB, provide:
- A link to the Permies.com thread about your location
- Picture of the sign hanging or posted at the location

Clarifications:
- No plywood, waferboard or particle board

☐ Brand a physical location
Complete 2:
  ☐ Upgrade a physical location that has already been branded (1.5 oddball points)
  ☐ Prepare a basic meal (and wash all the dishes) for at least 8 people
  ☐ Create (or update) a map showing the points of interest
  ☐ Teach a one hour workshop to 8 students
  ☐ Give a one hour presentation or tour to 8 participants
  ☐ Organize a flash flea market, collective garage sale or free swap
  ☐ Set up a Little Free Library
  ☐ Set up a free food stand
  ☐ Set up an honor system food stand

35 points required
  • Sand badge BBs are 1.5 points each
  • Up to 10 points of duplication allowed from the Straw badge
  • Up to 8 oddball points of community art allowed
☐ Create a community of 6 non-related people that lives together for 4 months and shares at least 1 meal a week - 15 points
  • Same 6 people for the same 4 months (can start and end with more than 6) are living on the same property
  • You create the community and entice the people to live there
☐ Community art - 2 to 4 oddball points
  • Needs to be in view of the community
☐ Brand a piece of equipment - 1 point
  • Give it a name and add some sort of interesting flair/character to the equipment
☐ Upgrade a physical location that has already been branded (2 to 4 oddball points)
☐ Create a private geocaching program and at least six points - 4 points
☐ Make a ceramic tile informational sign and mounting post - 2.5 points
  • 2 additional points if you made the tile from local clay
☐ Mount a "you are here" map on an existing structure - 1 point
☐ Create a "you are here" map structure - 1 to 15 points
  • 98% natural materials with protection from the elements
☐ Prepare a magnificent dinner (and wash all the dishes) for at least 8 people - 4 points
☐ Give a 2 hour presentation/tour - 1 to 5 points
☐ Arrange for 6 hours of presentations/tours - 2 to 10 points
☐ Teach a 1.5 hour workshop - 1 to 5 points
☐ Teach a 6 hour workshop - 2 to 10 points
  • Can be combined with "set up a 6 hour workshop" to get two BBs
☐ Set up a six hour workshop - 2 to 10 points
  • Can be combined with "teach a 6 hour workshop" to get two BBs

Sand badge

Free produce!

Straw badge

Carrie

permies.com/tour

- ☐ Improving a library - up to 4 oddball points
- ☐ Create and lead a work party - 1 to 10 points
  - 4 unrelated people and it doesn't have to be a public thing
- ☐ Hold an award ceremony for something and have at least 8 attendees - 2 points
  - If you make a physical award/trophy/badge - 1 more point
- ☐ Organize a group field trip with at least 6 attendees - 1 to 3 points
- ☐ Create a seed library - 2 to 12 points
  - At least 12 edible species and at least 12 packets of each species in a dry semi-secure location
  - At least 8 people check out packets

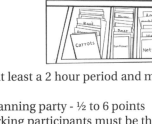

- ☐ Run a seed swap - ½ to 5 points
- ☐ Run a seedling swap - ½ to 5 points
- ☐ Start a club - 2 to 12 points
- ☐ Set up a cider pressing party - ½ to 6 points
  - The working participants must be there for at least a 2 hour period and make at least 4 gallons of cider

- ☐ Set up a canning party - ½ to 6 points
  - The working participants must be there for at least a 2 hour period and make at least 20 quarts or 30 pints
- ☐ Set up a chicken plucker party - ½ to 6 points
  - The working participants must be there for at least a 2 hour period and process at least 20 birds
- ☐ Create a self guided tour with 12 points of interest - 6 points

- ☐ Create a holiday (which could become annual) - 4 points
  - 1 more point if it's a winter holiday
  - 1 more point if crafting is involved
  - 1 more point if physical activity is involved
  - 1 more point for a theme related meal
  - 6 more points if the holiday is even better on year #2 (submit to the same BB thread for these points on year 2)
  - You are the master of ceremonies, orchestrating the holiday to be fun for everybody and it lasts 3 hours
  - Need at least 8 people for all events throughout the period and there are at least 4 or more unique events/activities/traditions
- ☐ Create a LIC (labor investment collective) - 4 points
  - 6 more points if the LIC lives on past your contributions
  - At least three artifacts are created (one for you) with at least six people participating
    - Must be for a BB and all artifacts are relatively similar for each participant
  - Check out chapter 53 for more about LICs

Knapweed Day

August 1

Wood badge

180 points required

- Up to 50 points of duplication allowed from the Wood, Straw and Sand badges
- New items from Sand and Straw badges allowed
- Sand badge BBs are worth 1.5 points

☐ Create a community of 6 non-related people that lives together for 6 months and shares at least 1 meal a week - 50 points
  - Same 6 people for the same 6 months (can start and end with more than 6) living on the same property
  - You create the community and entice the people to live there

☐ Community art - 5 to 40 oddball points

☐ Upgrade a physical location that has already been branded (5 to 20 oddball points)

☐ Create a food coop - 12 points
  - At least 8 members ordering food, making a bulk order, divvying it up and distributing it

☐ Create a recurring farmers market or flea market - 10 to 20 points
  - 5 or more sellers, 5 or more non-sellers (shoppers) and at least three market days

☐ Build a community garden - 20 to 50 points
  - At least 8 garden plots clearly marked out and labelled along with water, fencing, paths, rules and a shed. Occupying at least ½ acre.

☐ Manage a community garden for a year - 12 to 32 points
  - At least 8 gardeners

☐ Manage a seed library - 20 points
  - Prerequisite is Create a seed library BB or adopt an existing seed library
  - System to maintain "true to type" seeds, semi-secure seed storage with good signage and seed saving info and hold one informational program
  - At least 6 people return good seed and 8 check out seed with a total of at least 400 seed packets

☐ Create and lead a work party - 4 to 25 points
  - At least 6 hours of work and it doesn't have to be a public thing

☐ Facilitate a two day educational event/workshop/class - 10 to 30 points
  - Minimum 8 students at any time during the event, at least 16 hours of instruction and at least one meal provided per day

☐ Facilitate a one week educational event/workshop/class - 20 to 60 points
  - Minimum 8 students at any time during the event, at least 40 hours of instruction, at least 5 days and at least one meal provided per day

☐ Facilitate a two week educational event/workshop/class - 30 to 90 points
- For example: PDC, PDJ, SKIP event, etc.
- Minimum 8 students at any time during the event, at least 80 hours of instruction, at least 12 days and at least one meal provided per day

☐ Set up a fair - 20 to 40 points
- For example: Earth Day, Blue Grass music, Art, Harvest Fest, Fancy flea market, etc.
- At least 200 attendees, at least 6 vendors/booths, at least 2 presenters/workshops/artists/scheduled singers and at least 1 food option

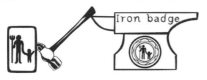

PEP
Community
Living

☐ Create a community of 8 non-related people that lives together for 30 months and shares at least 1 meal a week
- Same 8 people for the same 30 months (can start and end with more than 8) living on the same property
- You create the community and entice the people to live there

---

Sample Sand Badge BB:
Prepare and clean up a basic meal for 8 people

Minimum requirements:
- Prepare all the food for 8 people
- Clean up all the dishes, pots and pans, etc. used to cook and serve the food

This BB is tricky because the 8 people will try to help out. But the point is that you're doing all the work so that they can just enjoy themselves and build community.

Provide proof of the following as pictures or video (<2 mins):
- Post a list of all the foods you are serving, and say how many people you served
- The food being prepared
- The 8 people eating your food (we assume you are person #9 behind the camera)
- The dishes being cleaned up
- Clean kitchen and dining area

Sample Sand Badge BB:
Teach a 1 hour workshop

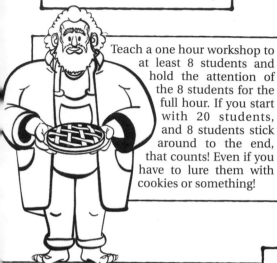

Teach a one hour workshop to at least 8 students and hold the attention of the 8 students for the full hour. If you start with 20 students, and 8 students stick around to the end, that counts! Even if you have to lure them with cookies or something!

Provide proof of the following as pictures or video (<2 mins):
- The workshop (with countable attendees) as it is beginning (including a clock or phone with the time)
- The workshop (with countable attendees) as it is ending (including a clock or phone with the time)
- You teaching the workshop with at least one identifiable attendee
- Some students doing a workshop activity

Sample Sand Badge BB:
Build an honor system food stand

Nothing shows that you welcome and love your community like a pile of unguarded food with a bucket of loose money next to it.

Provide proof of the following as pictures or video (<2 mins):
- Materials for the build
- Partway through the build
- Finished honor system food stand
- Demonstrate that people actually use the honor system food stand

Minimum requirements:
- Set up an honor system food stand
  - Could be indoors for communal kitchens
  - Could be for garden surplus

Textiles

"I noticed that he was freshly shaved and all his buttons were firmly sewed on, and that his clothes were donned with that meticulous care which makes a mend invisible."

-- Jean Giono
from "The Man Who Planted Trees" as we first encounter the hero, Elzéard Bouffier

Thanks to Raven from Crowing Hen Farm and Opalyn Rose for developing the majority of this aspect.

Mending shoes, upholstery, tents – creating clothes, mattresses or even a full, proper yurt from scratch – these are all skills that are part of the foundation of being a well-rounded homesteader.

Everything in this aspect requires natural materials preferring local/home-grown/harvested materials over anything purchased from a store. Natural fabrics or threads include cotton, wool, silk, linen/flax, and nettle. Natural materials for buttons or closures include mother-of-pearl, bone, horn, glass, metal, wood, and cloth. Synthetic materials are not allowed – even if they are recycled or repurposed.

PEP

Textiles

To document your completion, provide proof of the following as pics or video (<2 minutes):
- Your cotton yarn and crochet hook (or knitting needles)
- Dishcloth in progress
- Completed dishcloth
- Show it measures about 10 by 10 inches

Featured Sand Badge BB: Crochet or knit a dishcloth

In this project, you will crochet or knit a dishcloth out of cotton or other durable, natural absorbent fiber, like linen or hemp. It must measure about 10 by 10 inches.

Sand badge

☐ Mend a hole - quick darning
☐ Sew a patch
☐ Make a small pillow
☐ Make twine
☐ Weave a basket

Stickwork - complete 1:
  ☐ Knit or crochet a hot pad
  ☐ Crochet or knit a dishcloth

- ☐ Start a button jar
- ☐ Harvest fabric scraps for future sewing projects
  - ☐ Sew on a button
- ☐ Create a textile toolbox or hussif (sewing kit)

Mend a hole - invisible mending - complete 1

- ☐ Re-create knit fabric (possibly a sock) with knit-stitch darn
- ☐ Reinforce woven fabric where it is thinning or weak (starting to make a hole)
- ☐ Invisible mending a small hole or tear in the fabric
- ☐ Add a patch to torn fabric so that it is invisible from the outside (kaketsugi)
- ☐ Sewing machine maintenance
- ☐ Make a small loom capable of weaving a belt

31 points required

Repairs list - complete at least 3 points:

- ☐ Patch or darn a blanket (prettily) - ½ point
- ☐ Mend a hole in a coat - 1 point
- ☐ Mend a hole in a shirt or sleeve - ½ point
  - ☐ Mend hole in pants or skirt - ½ point
  - ☐ Mend a hole in a pocket - ½ point
- ☐ Mend pinhole tears in fabric - ½ point
- ☐ Mend damaged lining fabric in a garment - ½ point
- ☐ Mend a hole in a quilt - ½ point
- ☐ Mend a hole in a blanket - ½ point
- ☐ Mend a hole in a sweater - ½ point
- ☐ Mend/darn a hole in a sock - ½ point
- ☐ Mend a hole in a shoe or slipper - ½ point
- ☐ Mend a hole in a hat - ½ point
- ☐ Mend a hole in a mitten or glove - ½ point
- ☐ Fix a worn buttonhole - ½ point
- ☐ Remove pills from clothes - ½ point
- ☐ Hem trousers or skirt - 1 point
  - ☐ Turn trousers into shorts - 1 point
  - ☐ Add pockets to skirt or pants - ½ point
  - ☐ Replace the elastic or drawstring on the waistband of pants/skirt - 1 point
- ☐ Alter the waist on skirt or pants to fit - 1 point

- ☐ Replace the crotch in a pair of pants - 1.5 points
- ☐ Conceal a stain to make a garment look nice again - ½ point
- ☐ Add a gusset to a garment (eg underarms or crotch) to make it fit better - 1 point
- ☐ Add a panel to a shirt or dress to make it bigger - 1 point
- ☐ Add a panel to trousers or a skirt to make it bigger - 1 point
- ☐ Take in a shirt or dress to make it smaller - 1 point
- ☐ Take in trousers or a skirt to make it smaller - 1 point
- ☐ Add belt loops or suspender buttons to a pair of pants/trousers - ½ point
- ☐ Remove damaged or unwanted embroidery from a garment without damaging the garment - ½ point
- ☐ Unravel old sweater into yarn for other projects - 1 point
- ☐ Hem drapes/curtains (so that both curtains are the same length) - 1 point
- ☐ Sew the handles back onto a cloth bag, reinforcing as necessary - ½ point
- ☐ Fix hole or stitching in leather gloves/mittens - 1 point

- ☐ Fix hole or stitching on leather shoes/sandals - 1 point
- ☐ Fix hole or stitching on a leather bag/briefcase/suitcase/laptop bag - 1 point
- ☐ Fix hole or stitching on a leather coat - 1 point
- ☐ Repair stitching on a leather belt - 1 point
- ☐ Full leather maintenance on shoes, boots, or sandals - 2 points
- ☐ Full leather maintenance for leather gloves/mittens - ½ point
- ☐ Full leather maintenance for leather bag/briefcase/suitcase/laptop bag - ½ point
- ☐ Full leather maintenance for leather coat - ½ point

Upholstery list - complete at least 2 points:
- ☐ Repair a small hole in a couch, love seat, or padded chair - 1 point
- ☐ Patch a hole in a couch, love seat, or padded chair - 1 point
- ☐ Repair a tear (over 2 inches) in a couch, love seat, or padded chair - 2 points
- ☐ Add new fabric over the worn fabric on a padded chair - 1 point
- ☐ Add a permanent upholstery cushion to a chair or stool - 2 points
- ☐ Repair a small hole in a fabric seat in a car - 1 point
- ☐ Patch a hole in a fabric seat in a car - 1 point
- ☐ Repair a tear (over 2 inches) in a fabric seat in a car - 2 points

Bedding list - complete at least 2 points:
- ☐ Sew two sheets and two pillowcases (for twin size bed or larger) - 1 point
- ☐ Duvet cover - 1 point
- ☐ Quilted pillowcase - 2 points
- ☐ Quilted baby blanket - 3 points
- ☐ Make a firm, four-button pillow - 2 points
- ☐ Make a bolster pillow - 2 points
- ☐ Make two pillows for sleeping (natural stuffing) - 3 points

Weaving list - complete at least 3 points:
- ☐ Weave a belt - 2.5 points
- ☐ Weave a leash for a dog, goat, or other animal - 2 points
- ☐ Weave a camera strap - 2 points
- ☐ Weave a cotton or linen hand towel - 4 points
- ☐ Weave a small bag or purse - 3 points
- ☐ Weave a baby blanket (30 inches x 30 inches or larger) - 4 points
- ☐ Weave a blanket for a twin size bed or larger (65 inches x 90 inches or larger) - 5 points
- ☐ Basket weaving - seedling protection basket - 2 points
- ☐ Basket weaving - trash basket - 2.5 points
- ☐ Basket weaving - grocery basket - 6 points
- ☐ Basket weaving - harvest basket - 5 points
- ☐ Repair caning on a chair (small repair) - 1 point
- ☐ Replace caning on a chair (pre-woven caning) - 3 points
- ☐ Cane a chair (not pre-woven caning) - 6 points
- ☐ Repair weaving on a chair - 1 point
- ☐ Weave the seat of a chair or stool - 6 points

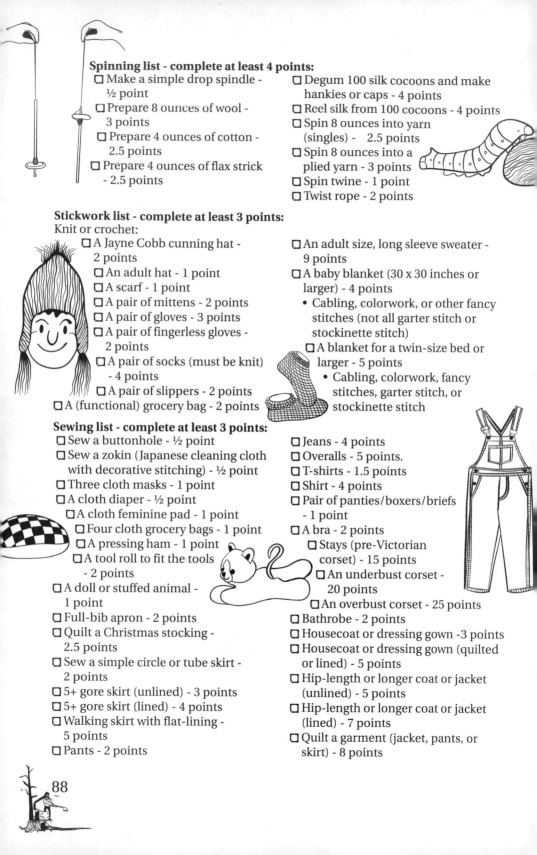

Spinning list - complete at least 4 points:

- ☐ Make a simple drop spindle - ½ point
- ☐ Prepare 8 ounces of wool - 3 points
- ☐ Prepare 4 ounces of cotton - 2.5 points
- ☐ Prepare 4 ounces of flax strick - 2.5 points
- ☐ Degum 100 silk cocoons and make hankies or caps - 4 points
- ☐ Reel silk from 100 cocoons - 4 points
- ☐ Spin 8 ounces into yarn (singles) - 2.5 points
- ☐ Spin 8 ounces into a plied yarn - 3 points
- ☐ Spin twine - 1 point
- ☐ Twist rope - 2 points

Stickwork list - complete at least 3 points:

Knit or crochet:

- ☐ A Jayne Cobb cunning hat - 2 points
- ☐ An adult hat - 1 point
- ☐ A scarf - 1 point
- ☐ A pair of mittens - 2 points
- ☐ A pair of gloves - 3 points
- ☐ A pair of fingerless gloves - 2 points
- ☐ A pair of socks (must be knit) - 4 points
- ☐ A pair of slippers - 2 points
- ☐ A (functional) grocery bag - 2 points
- ☐ An adult size, long sleeve sweater - 9 points
- ☐ A baby blanket (30 x 30 inches or larger) - 4 points
  - Cabling, colorwork, or other fancy stitches (not all garter stitch or stockinette stitch)
- ☐ A blanket for a twin-size bed or larger - 5 points
  - Cabling, colorwork, fancy stitches, garter stitch, or stockinette stitch

Sewing list - complete at least 3 points:

- ☐ Sew a buttonhole - ½ point
- ☐ Sew a zokin (Japanese cleaning cloth with decorative stitching) - ½ point
- ☐ Three cloth masks - 1 point
- ☐ A cloth diaper - ½ point
- ☐ A cloth feminine pad - 1 point
- ☐ Four cloth grocery bags - 1 point
- ☐ A pressing ham - 1 point
- ☐ A tool roll to fit the tools - 2 points
- ☐ A doll or stuffed animal - 1 point
- ☐ Full-bib apron - 2 points
- ☐ Quilt a Christmas stocking - 2.5 points
- ☐ Sew a simple circle or tube skirt - 2 points
- ☐ 5+ gore skirt (unlined) - 3 points
- ☐ 5+ gore skirt (lined) - 4 points
- ☐ Walking skirt with flat-lining - 5 points
- ☐ Pants - 2 points
- ☐ Jeans - 4 points
- ☐ Overalls - 5 points.
- ☐ T-shirts - 1.5 points
- ☐ Shirt - 4 points
- ☐ Pair of panties/boxers/briefs - 1 point
- ☐ A bra - 2 points
- ☐ Stays (pre-Victorian corset) - 15 points
- ☐ An underbust corset - 20 points
- ☐ An overbust corset - 25 points
- ☐ Bathrobe - 2 points
- ☐ Housecoat or dressing gown -3 points
- ☐ Housecoat or dressing gown (quilted or lined) - 5 points
- ☐ Hip-length or longer coat or jacket (unlined) - 5 points
- ☐ Hip-length or longer coat or jacket (lined) - 7 points
- ☐ Quilt a garment (jacket, pants, or skirt) - 8 points

Wax or oilcloth list

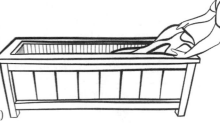

- ☐ Create 3 wax or oilcloths for food storage - 1 point
- ☐ Create wax or oilcloth and use it to make a lunch bag - 1.5 points
- ☐ Transform 1 yard of fabric into oilcloth - 2 points
- ☐ Sew a shoulder bag from oilcloth - 2 points
- ☐ Sew a rucksack from oilcloth - 5 points
- ☐ Sew a poncho from oilcloth - 3 points
- ☐ Sew a raincoat from oilcloth - 8 points

Dye list

- ☐ No-mordant dyeing - dye 2 lbs (dry weight) using no-mordant dyeing method - 2 points
- ☐ Natural mordant dyeing - dye 2 lbs (dry weight) using natural mordant dyeing method (alum okay) - 2.5 points
- ☐ Fermentation dyeing - dye 2 lbs (dry weight) using fermentation method - 4 points

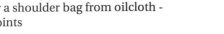

Felt list

- ☐ Felt a pouch or purse - 2 points
- ☐ Needle felt a figure - plant, animal, mythical, etc. - 1 point
- ☐ Wet felt a scarf - 1 point
- ☐ Wet felt a hat - 2 points
- ☐ Wet felt 3 wool dryer balls - 1 point

Leatherwork and fur list

- ☐ Leather thimble - ½ point
- ☐ Leather belt - 1 point
- ☐ Wallet - 3 points
- ☐ Hatchet or ax head protector - 1.5 points
- ☐ Knife sheath - 1.5 points
- ☐ Work gloves - 5 points
- ☐ Apron - 2 points
- ☐ Watch strap - 1 point
- ☐ Simple leather-bound notebook - 2 points
- ☐ Pruning shears holster - 1.5 points
- ☐ Tool pouch or roll - 3 points
- ☐ Tool belt with two pockets - 3 points
- ☐ Simple soft-soled shoes/slippers - 3 points
- ☐ Handbag/satchel - 3 points
- ☐ Backpack - 6 points
- ☐ Camera bag - 5 points
- ☐ Cured fish skin wallet - 4 points

Wood badge

- ☐ Patchwork quilt
- ☐ Make a camping cot-size mattress (tick) stuffed with natural materials

89

Seed list - complete one item and start from seed:

- ☐ Sew long underwear (top and bottom or one-piece) for cold weather
- ☐ Sew a long-sleeved woven shirt - button or pullover
- ☐ Create a short sleeve or sleeveless shirt
- ☐ Knit or crochet a sweater or cardigan
- ☐ Sew long pants, jeans, overalls, a skirt, or dress
- ☐ Create a full-bib apron or substantial tool belt
- ☐ Sew a winter coat (to keep you warm and dry all day at sub-freezing temperatures)
- ☐ Knit eight pairs of socks
  - Foundation garments (pick one):
    - ☐ Sew eight pairs of men's underwear
    - ☐ Sew two pairs of women's underwear and 1 support garment
      - Panties and shift, drawers and chemise, or combinations
      - Bra, stays, or a corset

125 points required

- New items from the Straw badge are allowed

Wardrobe list
Complete a full outfit

- Using the Straw BBs from the Sewing, Stickwork, Felting, and Leatherwork lists
- If you made the items to get your Straw badge, you don't need to repeat
- Including the following:
  - Undergarments
  - Socks
  - Woven or knit shirt or sweater
  - Pants, jeans, overalls, or skirt

Complete the Straw Dye list

- ☐ No-mordant dyeing - dye 2 lbs (dry weight) using no-mordant dyeing method - 2 points
- ☐ Natural mordant dyeing - dye 2 lbs (dry weight) using natural mordant dyeing method (alum okay) - 2.5 points
- ☐ Fermentation dyeing - dye 2 lbs (dry weight) using fermentation method - 4 points

Shoe list - complete 1:
- ☐ Hard-sole shoes - 12 points
- ☐ Hard-sole boots - 12 points

Big upholstery list - complete 1:
- ☐ Make a couch - 35 points
- ☐ Make a comfy chair (one person sofa) - 25 points

Small shelter list - complete 1:
- ☐ Oilcloth tarp (at least 12 x 14 feet) - 5 points
- ☐ Replace the canvas on a marquee tent, shelter frame, or easy up - 15 points
- ☐ Sleeping tent for 2+ people (at least 64 feet square footprint) - 10 points
- ☐ 10 x 10 foot open tent with removable walls or bug screens - 8 points

Big shelter list - complete 1:
- ☐ Yurt - 100 points
- ☐ Teepee - 50 points
- ☐ Canvas tent - 25 points
- ☐ Event tent (or event canopy with walls) - 45 points

Housewares list - complete 1:
- ☐ Make kitchen towels - 2 dish towels and 2 dishcloths - 15 points
- ☐ Make bath towels - 1 towel and 1 washcloth - 15 points
- ☐ Make a rug - 25 points
- ☐ Make privacy drapes - 8 points
- ☐ Make winter wool drapes - 8 points

- ☐ Sew a vegan winter coat and review your experience - 30 points
  - 4-hour stint outside at temperatures below freezing

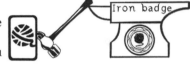

- ☐ Make a mattress with compressed stuffing
- ☐ Make a different Big Upholstery item than the one you made for the Wood badge
- ☐ Make a different shelter than the one you made for the Wood Big Shelter list

Complete the Seed list
- You do not need to repeat the item you completed at the Wood level
- You only need to complete one foundation garment BB

Make footwear, this time from seed.
Do not repeat the one you made for the Wood level Shoe list:
- ☐ Hard-soled shoes
- ☐ Hard-soled boots

Make three different housewares, this time from seed.
Do not repeat the one you made for the Wood Housewares list:
- ☐ Make kitchen towels - 2 dish towels and 2 dishcloths
- ☐ Make bath towels - 1 towel and 1 washcloth
- ☐ Make a rug (24 square feet)
- ☐ Make privacy drapes
- ☐ Make winter wool drapes

Sample Sand Badge BB:
Quick darning

In this project, you will mend a hole using quick darning.

To document your completion, provide proof of the following as pics or video (<2 minutes):
- Your holey cloth, darning needles, thread/yarn
- Darning in process
- Your no-longer-holey cloth
- It doesn't have to be pretty, it just has to be functional and not too bulky

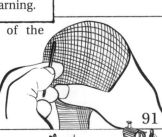

91

PEP

Textiles

Sample Sand Badge BB: Make twine

In this project, you will make twine from local plant material like nettles or suitable grasses.

To complete this Badge Bit, you must:
- Make at least a 20 foot length of twine
- The twine must be plyed

To document your completion, provide proof of the following as pics or video (<2 minutes):
- Raw materials
- Your process of making twine
- Your completed twine

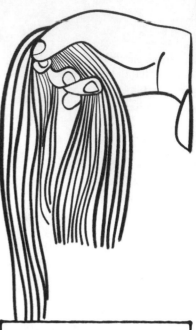

Sample Sand Badge BB: Sew a patch

In this project, you will sew a patch onto one of the following:
- An elbow of a shirt
- The knee of pants
- A quilt
- Tote bag
- Other woven fabric

To document your completion, provide proof of the following as pics or video (<2 minutes):
- Your holey fabric, patch, thread, and needle or sewing machine.
- Your patch being sewn onto the fabric.
- Completed patched fabric.
- It doesn't have to be pretty but it does have to be functional. Finish the edges of the patch so it doesn't fray.

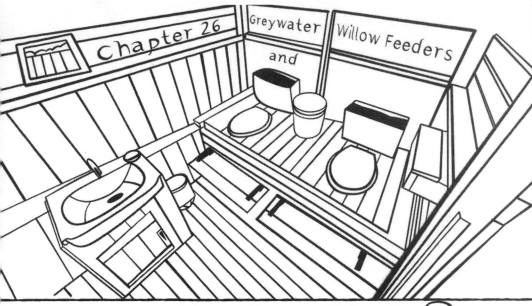

Modern sewage treatment plants are problematic. Liquids that enter the plant are typically released into our river systems within 24 hours and cause a lot of problems. The solids are separated and usually hauled to a dump. At the same time, there is a struggle to import nutrients for our horticultural practices.

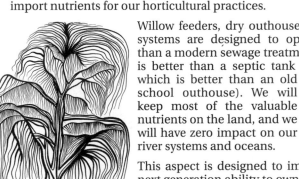

Willow feeders, dry outhouses and greywater systems are designed to operate far better than a modern sewage treatment plant (which is better than a septic tank and drain field, which is better than an old school outhouse). We will keep most of the valuable nutrients on the land, and we will have zero impact on our river systems and oceans.

PEP

Greywater & Willow Feeders

Thanks to Ash Jackson for developing a lot of substance for this aspect.

This aspect is designed to impress Otis with our powerful, next generation ability to own our own shit.

Featured Sand Badge BB: Create a level 1 pee spot

A small, new pee spot, with little privacy and relatively young plants

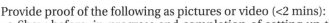

Pee here ⬇

Provide proof of the following as pictures or video (<2 mins):
- Show before, in-progress and completion of setting up the level one pee spot
- Provide proof that you've added two gallons of water to the pee spot at least once
- Clear imagery of the signage

Minimum requirements:
- Include a layer of wood chips on the ground, at least 18 inches in diameter, 2 inches deep
  - Could be a pre-existing mulch pit
    - Mulch pits are a different, Straw-level BB
- Plants must be a moderately established poop beast or urine-loving species that is active during the time the pee spot is in use
  - At least 3 plants total
  - Trees are at least 3 feet tall
  - Annual vines at least 3 feet long
  - Rhubarb at least 18 inches tall
- Include a can full of sawdust or wood chips within arm's reach
  - At least 20 gallons
  - With a lid that keeps the rain out
  - With a scoop
  - Can (or lid) is clearly labeled "sawdust" (or "wood chips")
- Include outdoor weather resistant signage that:
  - Has very large text, at the top that says "PEE HERE!"
  - Encourages people to diversify their urine placement all over the property, all over the sawdust in this pee spot and other pee spots
  - Cites at least 1 plant and describe the plant's ability to take up ample urine
  - Mentions that a bit of water from time to time will help the plants take up the urine
  - Instructs people that if the spot smells or there are flies, add more wood chips

Sand badge

- ☐ Plant five "poop beast" trees
- ☐ Use a bucket of water from a shower
- ☐ Use water from a dishpan
- ☐ Give urine to growies

Steinfeld list - complete 1:
- ☐ Significant art for a willow feeder or dry outhouse
  - ☐ Build a better urine diverter
    - Plus 1 point in Plumbing
    - Plus 5 points in Metalworking
    - ☐ Create a hand crafted, laminated information sheet
      - That details how a willow feeder works on one side
      - And how to deal with shark week on the other side
      - Lots of drawings

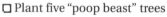

Welcome to the wonderful world of willow feeders

PEE OUTSIDE

Sprinkle sawdust generously

Close the lids/flaps

What happens to the willow candy

- ☐ Overhaul the ventilation system
- ☐ Overhaul the "occupied" system
- ☐ Seal a poorly sealed box on a willow feeder
- ☐ Urine diverter and sink drain to a mulch pit with a poop beast
- ☐ Dramatically improve the southern exposure for the Trombe wall
- ☐ Add a wood-burned, oil-sealed sign identifying the willow feeder
- ☐ Create a level 1 pee spot
  - Moderately established plants and signage

Willow Bank

Jenkins list - complete 2:

- ☐ Add art to a willow feeder or dry outhouse
- ☐ Move one willow feeder can to a willow candy warehouse
- ☐ Move one aged willow feeder can to a willow tree
- ☐ Improve the urine diverter
- ☐ Build a secondary fly trap
  - ☐ Empty a fly catcher that is at least 20% full
  - ☐ Improve a fly catcher
- ☐ Improve or repair the ventilation system
- ☐ Add a wax bag dispenser (with bags) for anything that needs to be contained before going into the garbage can
- ☐ Add a small garbage can with a foot pedal operated lid
- ☐ Add a system for sterilized and dirty "pee things for women" with proper labels
- ☐ Improve the "occupied" system
- ☐ Add 4 coat hooks
- ☐ Add a chalkboard to the inside
- ☐ A thorough cleaning

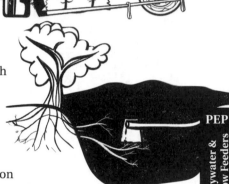

Straw badge

---

35 points required

- • New items from Sand badge allowed:
  - - Items on the Steinfeld list are worth 2 points
  - - Items on the Jenkins list are worth ½ point
- ☐ Build a small cold-climate greywater-fed mulch pit - 5 points
  - • 2 foot diameter by 4 foot deep hole, deposition chamber and plant two kinds of poop beasts
- ☐ Build a large cold-climate greywater-fed mulch pit - 10 points
  - • 4 foot diameter by 8 foot deep hole, deposition chamber and plant three kinds of poop beasts
- ☐ Plumb an outdoor sink to drain to a mulch pit - 2 points
- ☐ Plumb a greywater fixture (sink, shower, washer, etc.) to drain to a mulch pit - 4 points
- ☐ Plumb a greywater fixture (sink, shower, washer, etc.) to connect to an existing greywater drain - 2 points
- ☐ Take an existing greywater-fed mulch pit, and re-plumb the distribution so the greywater is split equally between two mulch pits - 3 points
  - • Show how you are making sure that the greywater is split roughly 50/50 (note that a simple "T" or "Y" often sends 90% or 100% of the flow down one path - so we need to see how you are preventing that)
- ☐ Reroute house plumbing that drains to a septic system drain field into a collection of mulch pits instead - 7 points
- ☐ Re-route a house that drains to a sewer system into a poor man's septic tank and then a collection of mulch pits instead - 7 points
- ☐ Build a poor man's septic tank for a greywater system - 5 points
- ☐ Create a level 2 pee spot - 4 points
  - • Established plants, very little privacy

PEP

Greywater &
Willow Feeders

95

- ☐ Create a level 3 pee spot - 6 points
  - Mature perennial plants, moderate privacy
- ☐ Create a level 4 pee spot - 8 points
  - Mature perennial plants, significant privacy, added privacy screen and moveable seat
- ☐ Upgrade a willow feeder or dry outhouse
  - Install a Trombe wall - 14 points
  - Build a truly great urine diverter - 8 points
    - Worthy of putting in a book, also get 5 points in metal working
  - Build a raised floor - 3 points
  - Urine diverter and sink drain goes to a mulch pit with a willow tree - 3 points
  - Oddball projects
    - Double points
- ☐ Build an indoor willow feeder - 20 points
  - ☐ Take a willow feeder to a fair/event for public use - 8 points
    - Available for use at least 8 hours with proof of happy customers
  - ☐ Build a willow candy warehouse - 16 points
  - ☐ Short experiments with willow candy - 14 points
    - Conduct experiments with 7 different willow candy cans for 12 weeks

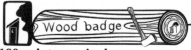

180 points required
- Up to 80 new points allowed from the Straw badge

- ☐ Build a dry outhouse (skiddable structure) - 40 points
- ☐ Build a outdoor willow feeder - 40 points
- ☐ Prove you've improved the quality of groundwater at a property - 60 points
- ☐ Wofati greenhouse that never freezes for processing greywater - 60 points
  - At least 6 feet x 8 feet inside with two thermal wells, wofati membrane and Oehler style cold sink
- ☐ Full-length experiments with willow candy - 50 points
  - Conduct experiments with 7 different willow candy cans for two years

No Iron badge at this time

Provide proof of the following as pictures or video (<2 mins):
- Show the tools and materials for improving the urine diverter
- Show before, progress, and after of improving the urine diverter in a willow feeder

Sample Sand Badge BB: Improve the urine diverter in a willow feeder

Sample Sand Badge BB:
Urine Diverter and Sink Drain to a Mulch Pit with a poop beast

Combine the output of the urine diverter and sink into a single pipe which feeds a mulch pit.

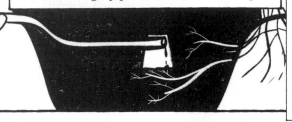

Provide proof of the following as pictures or video (<2 mins):
- Show the materials and tools used
- Show before, progress, and completion of creating a mulch pit with a poop beast
- Show before, progress, and completion of re-routing the urine diverter and sink drain

Sample Sand Badge BB:
Reuse water from a shower

Reuse water from a (sham)poo-less shower to flush a toilet or water something.

Minimum requirements:
- Place a bucket in your shower to collect some of the water as you (and others) shower
  - It might only collect 10% to 20% of the water, and that's okay for this BB
  - It might take a few days to get enough water
- Use the bucket of water to flush a toilet, or to water something outside
  - At least three gallons
  - From poo-less showers only!

Provide proof of the following as pictures or video (<2 mins):
- Three gallons of water from your shower that's obviously poo-less
- Giving the water to something outside or to flush a toilet

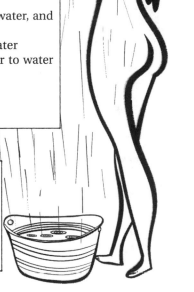

Chapter 27

Metalworking

Otis has a basic metal shop and is not shy about a bit of welding or grinding. He needs to know that you have at least a little experience. Are you able to repair the brush hog when needed? He's been thinking about re-mounting the jack on that old trailer – is that something you can do? He once made a nice latch for the barn – have you ever done anything like that?

Kindling crackers, whackers, splitters, bifurcators, etc. are very cool devices that can turn pieces of firewood into kindling.

Featured Sand Badge BB:
Build a kindling cracker

Minimum requirements:
- Cage accepts wood at least 8 inches in diameter (9 or more inches preferred)
- Bolted to a chopping block
  - Lots of knots in the block if it's a soft wood (possibly a taller than average chopping block)
  - The creation does not have to be centered on the chopping block
  - Stamp "made by XXXX" somewhere on it where XXXX is your name

Provide proof of the following as pictures or video (<2 mins):
- Your creation at two points of construction
- The finished product with a tape measure showing the the size of the wood that can enter
- The stamped name

Clarifications
- This is the metalworking badge so the part above the stump should be entirely made from metal

Sand badge

5 points required

- ☐ Build a kindling cracker - 4.5 points
  - ☐ Poker - ½ point
  - ☐ Tongs - ½ point
  - ☐ RMH scoop - ½ point
  - ☐ Metal rack to hold a poker, a set of tongs and a RMH scoop - ½ point
  - ☐ Make a twisting wrench - ½ point
  - ☐ Weld two hooks or chain clevises to a tractor bucket - ½ point
- ☐ Weld a trailer ball to a tractor implement - ½ point
- ☐ Beefy set of shelf brackets - 1 point
- ☐ Fix a crack in a tool - ½ point
- ☐ Marshmallow or hot dog fork for campfire - 1 point (2 if SS)
- ☐ Dress up a mushroomed chisel or splitting wedge - ½ point
- ☐ Make a center punch - ½ point
- ☐ Chicken funnel - ½ point
- ☐ Solar oven reflectors - ½ point

Welding list - complete at least seven points and at least 4 different items:

Projects should mainly be constructed by gas or arc welding

☐ Make a guillotine fuller - 3 points
☐ Make a spring fuller - 1 point
☐ Make four matching angle braces (broader than 90 degrees) to attach legs to a platform (deer stand, water tower, etc.) - 2 points
☐ Welded digging fork - 1 point
☐ Sawhorse brackets for two wooden sawhorses - 2 points
☐ Door latch - 1 point
☐ Make a gouge for making log bee houses - 1 point

Forging list - complete at least seven points and at least 5 different items:

Projects should mainly be constructed by forging

☐ Set of tongs with rivet and drawn out handles - 2 points
☐ Forge and heat treat two punches or hot chisels or one of each (show they aren't brittle) - 1 point
☐ Nice fire poker - 1 point
☐ Nice gate handle - 1 point
☐ Drawknife - 3 points
☐ Hardy hole tool - 1 point
☐ Forged digging fork - 3 points
☐ Forge a spring fuller - 1 point
☐ Log peeling spud - 2 points
☐ Tomahawk head from railroad spike (ready for handle) - 2 points
☐ Decent knife from railroad spike or file - 2 points

☐ Heat treat a homemade knife and prove it - 1 point
☐ Hand trowel - 2 points
☐ Hinge - 2 points
☐ Holdfast - 1 point
☐ 2 wingnuts or other hand tightened nuts - 2 points
☐ Repoint and harden/temper a pointy tool (pick, mattock, etc.) without removing any metal - 2 points
☐ 20 nails - 2 points
☐ Branding iron (for leather or wood) - 3 points
☐ Utility grade broad axe - 3 points
☐ Utility grade adze - 2 points
☐ Utility grade froe - 2 points
☐ Utility grade gouge - 2 points

Shop list - complete at least seven points and at least 4 different items:

☐ Crude forge - 1 point
☐ Prep coil spring to use for 6 punches/chisels - 1 point
☐ Crude anvil on a stump - 1 point
☐ Sturdy metal work table - 2 points
☐ Make a sheet metal hand brake - 1 point
☐ Rebar drawer/door handle (flattened ends) - 1 point
☐ Nail heading plate - 2 points
☐ Stamp with initials to mark metal - 2 points

PEP

Metalworking

Sheet metal list - complete at least seven points and at least 5 different items:

☐ Water trough or pan - 2 points
☐ Nice RMH ash scoop - 1 point
☐ Nice dustpan - 1 point
☐ Grain scoop - 1 point
☐ Squirrel/raccoon guard for a post - 1 point
☐ Pinwheel or spiral wind spinner to scare birds from growies - 1 point
☐ Chicken feeder - 2 points

☐ Sink a small bowl or spoon - 2-6 points
☐ Gravity powered fan - 2 points for Sheet Metal, 4 points for Other
☐ Lamp shade - 3 points
☐ Reflector style camp stove (redirects heat from campfire to cook) - 4 points
☐ Copper flower - 1 point

99

- ☐ Storage box without lid - 2 points
- ☐ Storage box with lid - 4 points
- ☐ Chimney cap - 4 points
- ☐ Berry picker hand scoop - 1 point
- ☐ Berry picker standing scoop - 2 points
- ☐ Mailbox - 2 points

Other list - complete at least seven points and at least 5 different items:

- ☐ Make, grind, polish and stamp a name tag or key fob - 1 point
- ☐ Solder some garden art (flowers, etc) from copper - ½-4 points
- ☐ Sand cast anything from aluminum (bigger than a golf ball) - 2 points
  - ☐ Cut a sign from metal, torch or plasma (8 inches by 18 inches min) - 1 point
    - ☐ Copper tongs - 2 points
- ☐ Copper shishi odoshi - 3 points
- ☐ Campfire tripod and hanging grill (buy grill and bulk chain, make/assemble the rest) - 2 points
- ☐ Assemble firearm from purchased components - 2 points
- ☐ Draw down the diameter of a piece of wire with a draw plate - 1 point
- ☐ Make a 6 oz ingot of metal other than lead - 2 points

180 points required
- Oddball points allowed

Wood badge

Welding list:

Projects should mainly be constructed by gas or arc welding, one project needs to be from metal other than steel

- At least 30 points required
- At least 3 new items from Straw list
- At least 4 items from this list:

  - ☐ Build a trailer (4x6 feet or bigger) - 8-24 points
  - ☐ Make a welding table - 8-16 points
  - ☐ Two matching metal sawhorses - 4 points
  - ☐ Work stand (vertically adjustable "T" that screws down into tripod legs) - 4 points
  - ☐ Exhaust system for a vehicle - 3-6 points
  - ☐ Make a length of chain with 10 links - 3 points
  - ☐ J tube rocket engine (twofer with Rocket badge) - 4 points
  - ☐ Decorative arbor or entry for a gate - 8-16 points
  - ☐ Functional gate - 4 points
  - ☐ Pretty gate - 8-16 points
  - ☐ Bicycle frame - 8 points

Forging list:
Projects should mainly be constructed by forging
- At least 30 points required
- At least 3 new items from Straw list
- At least 4 items from this list:
  - ☐ All the hardware for a door (hinges, latch, knob), no lock - 6-18 points
  - ☐ Custom hammer (hardened) - 2 points
  - ☐ Beautiful door knocker - 3-9 points
  - ☐ Beautiful door handle - 3-9 points
  - ☐ 10 punches/drifts/chisels - 3 points
  - ☐ Beautiful axe - 4-12 points
  - ☐ C-clamp - 4 points
  - ☐ Shovel - 6 points
  - ☐ Decorative and functional spindles for 10 feet of railing - 6-18 points
  - ☐ Make a length of chain with 10 links (forge welding) - 5 points
  - ☐ Soup ladle from one piece of metal (food safe) - 3 points
  - ☐ 1 place setting of tableware fork/knife/spoon (food safe) - 4-8 points
  - ☐ High quality broad axe - 4 points
  - ☐ High quality adze - 3 points
  - ☐ High quality froe - 3 points
  - ☐ High quality gouge - 3 points
  - ☐ Two person log tong (swivel or pinching)- 4 points

Sheet metal list:
- At least 30 points required
- At least 3 new items from Straw list
- At least 3 items from this list:
  - ☐ Custom bike fender - 4 points
  - ☐ Custom ductwork for hvac system (20') - 8 points
  - ☐ Raise a small bowl - 4-12 points
  - ☐ Watering can - 8-16 points
  - ☐ Copper pot/kettle/pan - 8-16 points (counts for Other or Forging)
  - ☐ Urine diverter for willow feeder - 5 points

Other list:
At least 30 points required
- At least 1 new item from Straw Shop list
- At least 1 new item from Straw Other list
- At least 4 items from this list:

  - ☐ Keyed lock - 8-24 points
  - ☐ Safe box that is pretty- 4-12 points
  - ☐ Make a gun barrel - 10 points
  - ☐ Make a firearm - 30-90 points
  - ☐ Smelt iron from ore - 50 points
  - ☐ Make a heat powered wood stove fan - 20 points
  - ☐ Veggie oil foundry - 4 points
  - ☐ Japanese box bellows - 8 points

  - ☐ Treadle hammer - 20 points
  - ☐ Build a welder - 8 points
  - ☐ Build a plasma cutter - 16 points
  - ☐ Nice cutting table - 8 points
  - ☐ Turn down a brake rotor - 2 points
  - ☐ Stamp with artistic touchmark to mark metal - 3 points
  - ☐ Timber tool - 16 points
  - ☐ Log arch - 12 points

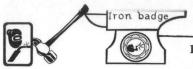
Iron badge

1030 points required
* Oddball points allowed

Welding list:
Projects should be primarily but not necessarily entirely constructed by welding.
* At least 100 points required
* At least 3 new items from Wood level
* More new items from Straw and Wood Welding lists allowed
* 1 project must be with aluminum and one with stainless steel.

☐ Hammer patch and weld a hole in a truck - 8 points
☐ Large smoker - 30 points
☐ Large trailer - 40 points
☐ Convert a vehicle to wood or charcoal gasification - 80 points
  * Street legal, capable of 60mph and 40 mile range
☐ Convert a tractor or garden tractor to wood gasification - 40 points
  * Capable of 6 hrs run time
☐ Small trailer with walking suspension - 40 points
☐ Large trailer with walking suspension - 60 points
☐ Large solar panel mounting system (braces, not just clips) 60+ square feet - 20 points

Forging list:
Projects should be primarily but not necessarily entirely constructed by forging.
* At least 100 points required
* At least 3 new items from Wood level
* More new items from Straw and Wood Forging lists allowed

☐ Beautiful fire tool set - 16-48 points
☐ Iron/steel gate (think 1700's Europe) - 80-240 points
☐ Elegant spindles for 10 feet railing - 12-36 points
☐ Chandelier - 40-120 points
☐ Nice candelabra or pair of candlesticks - 16 points
☐ Coach light - 8 points

Sheet metal list:
At least 100 points required
* More new items from Straw and Wood Sheet metal lists allowed
☐ Beautiful hammered copper sink (food safe) - 40 points
☐ Steel wok - 40 points

Other list:
At least 100 points required
* More new items from Straw and Wood Other lists and the Straw Shop list allowed
☐ Make a mid size lathe - 100 points
☐ Convert a vehicle to electric - 65 points
  * Street legal, capable of 60mph and 40 mile range
  * Also earns 40 points of Electricity
☐ Convert a motorcycle or dirt bike to electric - 12 points
  * Street legal, capable of 20 mile range
  * Also earns 20 points of Electricity

☐ Convert a tractor to electric - 65 points
- Capable of 6 hours run time
- Also earns 40 points of Electricity

☐ Large articulating solar panel system ala Solar Leviathan - 40 points
- 40+ square feet of panels
- Also earns 40 points of Electricity

Sample Sand Badge BB: Dress up a mushroomed chisel or splitting wedge

After a while, tools that you hit with a hammer can get mushroomed. Let's fix it!

Minimum requirements:
- Fix a mushroomed striking surface on tools like:
  - Chisel
  - Splitting wedge
  - Hammer
  - Punch

Provide proof of the following as pictures or video (<2 mins):
- The mushroomed head
- The repair in progress
- The fixed tool
- A description of how you repaired it

Sample Sand Badge BB: Build a RMH scoop

Scooping the ash out of a J-tube rocket mass heater can be challenging. This tool is not currently available for sale, so the only option to have this tool is to make one.

Minimum requirements:
- Steel, iron, aluminum or copper
- Must be designed to clean ash from the burn tunnel and lift it out the wood feed (may take multiple scoopings)
- Needs small edges on three of the sides to help lift ash out

Provide proof of the following as pictures or video (<2 mins):
- Your scoop partially assembled
- The finished scoop

Sample Straw Badge BB: Heat treat a homemade knife

Making a knife from a file or railroad spike is a cool project. The trick is hardening the knife enough to hold an edge while not getting it too brittle.

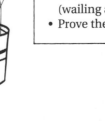

Provide proof of the following as pictures or video (<2 mins):
- Proof that the knife is homemade
- Partway through heat treating
- The finished heat treated homemade knife
- Cut something that proves the knife edge is hardened (wailing away on hardwood, etc.)
- Prove the knife is still sharp

Chapter 28

Plumbing and Hot Water

I wish there was a way to wander out into the woods and find stainless steel pipe growing on the stainless steel pipe tree. Then our plumbing systems could align with our permaculture values of natural building. Instead, we "make the best of it" and contemplate which paths are the least toxic.

Otis has deep respect for plumbing skills.

Featured Sand Badge BB:
Replace washing
machine supply hoses

Minimum requirements:
- Replace a pair of washing machine supply hoses

Provide proof of the following as pictures or video (<2 mins):
- Removing the old washing machine supply hoses
- Installing the new washing machine supply hoses

Tiny list - complete 6:
☐ Fix a leaky faucet
☐ Fix a leaky toilet
☐ Clean/decalcify a faucet aerator
☐ Repair a hose
☐ Unclog a drain with zip tool
☐ Repair a p-trap
☐ Repair a toilet that is not well bolted down
☐ Repair a toilet with problems with the lid/seat
☐ Install an "instant bidet" on a toilet
☐ Clean/decalcify a shower head
☐ Perform a water quality test
☐ Extract sediment from the cistern
☐ Prepare an outdoor shower for winter

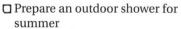

Sand badge

☐ Prepare an outdoor shower for summer
☐ Repair a hydrant
☐ Put collected water through a Berkey filter
☐ Flush the water heater
☐ Replace the anode in the water heater
☐ Replace washing machine supply hoses
☐ Replace a sump pump
☐ Set up a temporary water pump in a pond or water source
☐ Set up a siphon from a water source downhill to a location

Big list - complete 1:
- ☐ Install a hydrant
- ☐ Set up a sink with a foot pump
- ☐ Set up a solar water pump
  (combo with Electricity badge)
- ☐ Replace a faucet
- ☐ Replace or install a frost free spigot

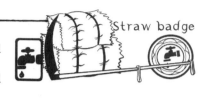

35 points required
- 10 points of duplication allowed from the Sand and Straw badge
- Up to 5 new points allowed from the Sand badge
  - Items on the Tiny list are worth ½ point
  - Items on the Big list are worth 1 point
- Plumbing oddball points allowed

Straw badge

Fix-it List:
- ☐ Fix a leak in a supply pipe - 1 point
- ☐ Fix a leak in a DWV pipe - 1 point
- ☐ Replace a toilet - 2 points
- ☐ Replace a pressure tank - 1 point
- ☐ Replace a sink - 1 point
- ☐ Replace a dishwasher - 1 point

Plumbing List:
- ☐ Install a water heater - 4 points
  - Combo with Electricity if it's electrically powered
- ☐ Install a dishwasher in a new location - 2 points
- ☐ Install a sump pump and permanent exit piping - 4 points
- ☐ Install a shallow well pump for potable pressurized water - 1-2 points
  - Combo with Electricity
- ☐ Install a deep well pump for potable pressurized water - 4-8 points
  - Combo with Electricity
- ☐ Install a control system and secondary pump for a cistern
  (not the main well) - 4-8 points
  - Combo with Electricity
- ☐ Extend a propane piping system to a new location - 2 points
- ☐ Install a valve in an existing pipe - 1 point
- ☐ Extend water supply piping to a new location - 1 point for hot, 1 point for cold
- ☐ Install a drain (with proper venting) to a new location - 4-8 points
- ☐ Trench water to a hydrant or outbuilding - 4 points
- ☐ Change an exterior faucet over to a frost proof style - 1 point

Make-it List:
- ☐ Make a water filter (like a Berkey water filter) - 1 point
- ☐ Make a simple sand filter - 1 point
- ☐ Build a permanent sand filter - 8 points
  - Handles floaters and sinkers and is plumbed into your system

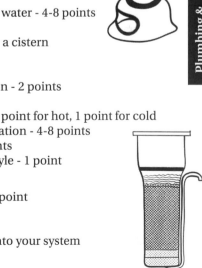

PEP

Plumbing & Hot Water

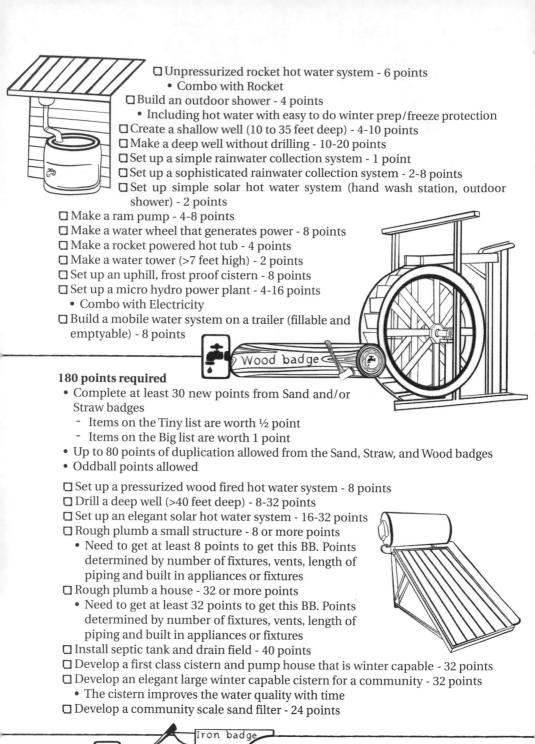

☐ Unpressurized rocket hot water system - 6 points
  • Combo with Rocket
☐ Build an outdoor shower - 4 points
  • Including hot water with easy to do winter prep/freeze protection
☐ Create a shallow well (10 to 35 feet deep) - 4-10 points
☐ Make a deep well without drilling - 10-20 points
☐ Set up a simple rainwater collection system - 1 point
☐ Set up a sophisticated rainwater collection system - 2-8 points
☐ Set up simple solar hot water system (hand wash station, outdoor shower) - 2 points
☐ Make a ram pump - 4-8 points
☐ Make a water wheel that generates power - 8 points
☐ Make a rocket powered hot tub - 4 points
☐ Make a water tower (>7 feet high) - 2 points
☐ Set up an uphill, frost proof cistern - 8 points
☐ Set up a micro hydro power plant - 4-16 points
  • Combo with Electricity
☐ Build a mobile water system on a trailer (fillable and emptyable) - 8 points

180 points required
  • Complete at least 30 new points from Sand and/or Straw badges
    - Items on the Tiny list are worth ½ point
    - Items on the Big list are worth 1 point
  • Up to 80 points of duplication allowed from the Sand, Straw, and Wood badges
  • Oddball points allowed

☐ Set up a pressurized wood fired hot water system - 8 points
☐ Drill a deep well (>40 feet deep) - 8-32 points
☐ Set up an elegant solar hot water system - 16-32 points
☐ Rough plumb a small structure - 8 or more points
  • Need to get at least 8 points to get this BB. Points determined by number of fixtures, vents, length of piping and built in appliances or fixtures
☐ Rough plumb a house - 32 or more points
  • Need to get at least 32 points to get this BB. Points determined by number of fixtures, vents, length of piping and built in appliances or fixtures
☐ Install septic tank and drain field - 40 points
☐ Develop a first class cistern and pump house that is winter capable - 32 points
☐ Develop an elegant large winter capable cistern for a community - 32 points
  • The cistern improves the water quality with time
☐ Develop a community scale sand filter - 24 points

No Iron badge at this time

Sample Sand Badge BB: Unclog a drain with a zip tool

Zip tools are a way to fix a clogged drain without nasty chemicals. It is a thin, flexible strip with barbs that you insert into the drain and pull out the obstructions.

Provide proof of the following as pictures or video (<2 mins):
- The clogged drain
- Using the zip tool on the clogged drain
- Your previously clogged drain, now draining properly

Minimum requirements:
- You must unclog a clogged drain, using a zip tool or something similar.

Sample Sand Badge BB: Clean/decalcify a shower head

Minimum requirements:
- Clean/decalcify a shower head

Provide proof of the following as pictures or video (<2 mins):
- Dirty/calcified shower head operating poorly
- Cleaning/decalcifying the shower head
- Newly cleaned/decalcified shower head operating properly
- A description of the method for how the shower head was cleaned/decalcified

Sample Sand Badge BB: Set up a solar water pump

This is a direct solar-to-pump scenario. Extremely simple. No batteries. DC only. When you have completed this one badge, it counts as a BB for both the electricity badge and the plumbing badge – you don't have to do it twice.

Holding water high in your landscape is a goal many of us strive for. If it doesn't naturally appear there, you might have to pump it up there. A solar pump will move the water up only when the sun shines. Sometimes, that's enough. This also helps to aerate water for aquatic life.

Provide proof of the following as pictures or video (<2 mins):
- The area where the pump and panel will be installed
- The pump and panel before you install/assemble them
- In-progress installation
- The completed installation
- Water coming out of the pipe
- Description of the materials and process, including how 5gpm was measured

Minimum requirements:
- Set up a solar water pump
  - No battery
  - Direct solar panel to pump
  - Minimum of 5 gallons per minute in full sun
  - Air lift technique is acceptable/preferred

1 point for a temporary test
- Something that can be put away after the BB is complete

2.5 points for a permanent installation
- At least 10 feet of head

Chapter 29

Electricity

Most of the world's problems are tied to energy use. At the same time, many of the greatest luxuries of our time are powered by electricity. To maximize your luxuriance and minimize your electrical footprint calls for experience with electricity.

Otis needs to know that you have experience with electrical stuff.

Featured Sand Badge BB: Create a micro heater bubble

It is possible to be quite comfortable by just heating your immediate surroundings instead of the entire room.

Minimum requirements:
- Create a microheater bubble
  - Document your comfort after one hour with the air temp at 60 degrees F
  - Optimize the bubble so you can be comfortable, sitting still, for three hours at 50 degrees F
  - Must have one incandescent directional light
    · Close to head, but not in your eyes
    · Light is not in the eyes of anybody
    · Easy to turn on and off
  - Must have a dog bed heater
    · A style that will not overheat
    · Easy to turn on and off
  - Must have a lap warmer
    · Couch or chair can just be a blanket
    · Desk must be a kotatsu
  - Desk must have
    · Heated pad under keyboard and mouse, or
    · Heated keyboard and heated mouse

To show you've completed this Badge Bit, you must provide:
- 2 minute video of you demonstrating the above requirements
- Provide a list of the microheaters you are using and where they are located in your heater bubble

Sand badge

5 points required

☐ Lead acid battery maintenance on three batteries - 1 point
☐ Create a micro heater bubble - 1 point
☐ Move a lead acid battery to the shop, charge it, and put it back - ½ point
☐ Replacing a bathroom fan switch with a timer - ½ point
☐ Repair a lamp (110v, 12v, car) - ½ point
☐ Repair a motion detector flood lamp - ½ point
☐ Replace a flood light with a motion detector flood lamp - ½ point

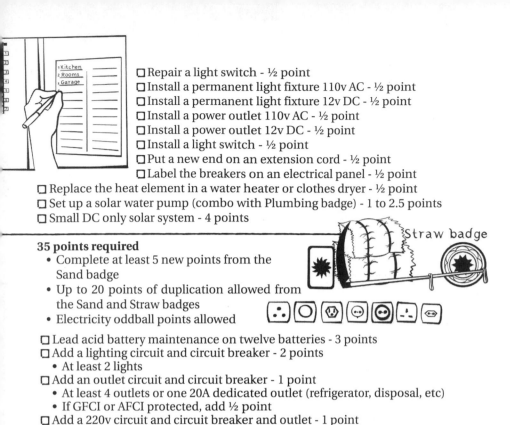

☐ Repair a light switch - ½ point
☐ Install a permanent light fixture 110v AC - ½ point
☐ Install a permanent light fixture 12v DC - ½ point
☐ Install a power outlet 110v AC - ½ point
☐ Install a power outlet 12v DC - ½ point
☐ Install a light switch - ½ point
☐ Put a new end on an extension cord - ½ point
☐ Label the breakers on an electrical panel - ½ point
☐ Replace the heat element in a water heater or clothes dryer - ½ point
☐ Set up a solar water pump (combo with Plumbing badge) - 1 to 2.5 points
☐ Small DC only solar system - 4 points

Straw badge

35 points required

- Complete at least 5 new points from the Sand badge
- Up to 20 points of duplication allowed from the Sand and Straw badges
- Electricity oddball points allowed

☐ Lead acid battery maintenance on twelve batteries - 3 points
☐ Add a lighting circuit and circuit breaker - 2 points
  - At least 2 lights
☐ Add an outlet circuit and circuit breaker - 1 point
  - At least 4 outlets or one 20A dedicated outlet (refrigerator, disposal, etc)
  - If GFCI or AFCI protected, add ½ point
☐ Add a 220v circuit and circuit breaker and outlet - 1 point
☐ Replace an electric water heater - 1 point
☐ Add a new circuit breaker and install a new electric water heater - 2 points
  - Combo with Plumbing
☐ Install a doorbell system (chime, transformer, button) - 1 point
☐ Install a shallow well pump for potable pressurized water - 1-2 points
  - Combo with Plumbing
☐ Install a deep well pump for potable pressurized water - 4-8 points
  - Combo with Plumbing
☐ Install a control system and secondary pump for a cistern - 4-8 points
  - Combo with Plumbing
☐ Install a pair of three way switches to control a light/device - 1 point
☐ Install a set of four way switches to control a device - 1.5 points
☐ Install an exterior grade outlet (code compliant cover) - 1 point
☐ Install an exterior grade outlet (Paul compliant cover) - 2 points
☐ Install 20 feet of wire in an unfinished space - 1 point
☐ Install 20 feet of wire to a finished space from an unfinished space - 1.5 point
☐ Install 20 feet of wire, flawlessly, through an existing finished wall - 4 points
☐ Install a subpanel with ground - 6 points
☐ Trench power to an outbuilding properly - 10 points
☐ Document electrical usage of 12 devices with a Kill-A-Watt - 2 points
☐ Troubleshoot and fix an electrical appliance - ½ to 4 points
☐ Set up an emergency back-up battery system that is always charged - 1 point
☐ "Charge and Carry" lithium battery power box - 20 points

- ☐ Augment a pickup (or other rig) to be a power generator with at least 2 batteries - 4 points
- ☐ Create a Travis Johnson style PTO driven home generator
  - Properly (to code) power a grid tied house for an hour - 12 points
  - Augment off-grid batteries - 2 points
  - Able to run certain appliances with a cord - 2 points
- ☐ Set up a power wall
  - Off-grid - 10 points
  - Grid-tied - 20 points
- ☐ Set up a micro hydro power system
  - Off-grid - 10 points
  - Grid-tied - 20 points
  - Combo with Plumbing
- ☐ Set up a wind power system
  - Off-grid - 10 points
  - Grid-tied - 20 points

180 points required
- Up to 35 points of duplication allowed from the Sand, Straw and Wood badges
- Up to 60 new points allowed from the Straw and Sand badges
- Electricity oddball points allowed

- ☐ Fully wire a small structure with a single supply wire - 4 or more points
  - Need to get at least 4 points to get this BB. Points come from the number of outlets, switches and fixtures with bonuses for exterior and GFCI/AFCI applications
- ☐ Fully wire a small structure with 3+ circuits (panel installed already) - 12 or more points
  - Need to get at least 12 points to get this BB. Points come from the number of outlets, switches and fixtures with bonuses for exterior and GFCI/AFCI applications
- ☐ Fully wire a large structure with 6+ circuits (panel installed already) - 40+ points
  - Need to get at least 40 points to get this BB. Points come from the number of outlets, switches and fixtures with bonuses for exterior and GFCI/AFCI applications
  - Properly illuminated, at least two outlets outside and at least one 220v outlet
- ☐ Install a main panel, meter pedestal, ground and connect their wiring - 15 points
- ☐ Convert a vehicle to electric - 40 points
  - Street legal, capable of 60mph and 40 mile range
  - Also earns 65 points in Metalworking (Iron)
- ☐ Convert a motorcycle or dirt bike to electric - 20 points
  - Street legal, capable of 20 mile range
  - Also earns 12 points in Metalworking (Iron)
- ☐ Convert a tractor to electric - 40 points
  - Capable of 6 hrs run time
  - Also earns 65 points in Metalworking (Iron)
- ☐ Troubleshoot and repair an electrical issue with an electrically powered vehicle - 2 to 20 points
  - Electric car, golf cart, tractor, motorcycle, etc
- ☐ Large articulating solar panel system (40+ square feet) - 40 points
  - Also earns 40 points in Metalworking (Iron)

No Iron badge at this time

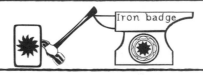

Sample Sand Badge BB: Replace a bathroom fan switch with a timer

Minimum requirements:
• Replace a bathroom fan switch with a timer

Provide proof of the following as pictures or video (<2 mins):
• Existing bathroom fan switch and the timer you will install
• During the install
• The completed install

Sample Sand Badge BB: Put a new end on an extension cord

Minimum requirements:
• Put a new end on an extension cord, build an extension cord or replace the end on a tool's cord.

Provide proof of the following as pictures or video (<2 mins):
• Before
• During the project
• Repaired cord

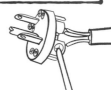

Sample Sand Badge BB: Small DC only solar system

Provide proof of the following as pictures or video (<2 mins):
• Description of the system, power and capacity
• Explain how the battery(s) will put out 100W for 6 hours
• Area where the system will be installed
• Parts before you install/assemble them
  • Completed installation
    • Evidence of a phone charging

Side Notes:
• If you have an alternative solar installation that you'd like to do of a similar complexity, post to the BB thread on Permies.com and ask if it could be added as an option.

Minimum requirements:
• Choose one of the following systems to build:
  - Small solar music cart and phone charging station
    · Includes 12v Bluetooth speakers hard wired
  - Small DC system on a shed: lights and phone charging
  - Tiny home power system: lights, phone charging, outlets
  - RV or camping power system: lights and phone charging
• Must have at least one 12v outlet
• Must have at least one 5v USB outlet
• Must include a charge controller
• Must include a battery
  - Must be able to put out 100 watts for 6 hours.

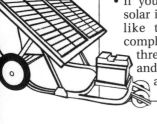

This aspect has a strong focus on reassuring Otis that you will not simply cash out what you inherit – even when times get tough.

Otis is looking for somebody who will have a relationship with his land, all day, 365 days a year. Not somebody who leaves for 40 hours a week. Nor somebody who leaves for even one day a week for a job (or managing a booth at the farmer's market). A dedicated, on-site relationship with the land.

Demonstrate the ability to be financially self-sufficient without leaving the land.

Featured Sand Badge BB: Develop a possible residual income stream

Develop a possible residual income stream that brings in at least $5 per year

To get certified for this BB, post the following:
- A description of your income stream and how this will continue to bring in an income for at least a few years
- A link to it
- A picture of proof it made $1.99 or more (you can smudge out the personal info, so long as it is identifiable as you)

Minimum requirements:
- Must bring in at least $1.99 before this BB is complete
- Describe how this will continue to bring in an income for at least a few years
- Do something where if you went to the middle of the ocean for a year, you'd come back and your bank account grew
- For purposes of PEP, it must be something you developed
  - Product development, residuals, royalties and pensions count
  - Not something you bought your way into (investment, dividend, CD, etc.)
  - Not something that happened to you (insurance claim, accident payout, inheritance, etc.)

Purpose: Show Otis that you will arrive with some income and different income skills

☐ Develop a possible residual income stream that brings in at least $5 per year
☐ Perform some sort of labor over the internet and get paid at least $50

Do two of the following: (must include a tip of the hat to permaculture values)

❑ Sell "goods" (something you made, grew, upcycled or foraged) for a total of at least $20

❑ Sell your permaculture labor off-site for at least $50

❑ Get paid for an on-homestead service (cottage industry) for at least $50

- Examples include:
  - Renting out a cabin, tent site, etc.
    - Sewing, truck repair, accounting, etc.
      - Massage, counseling, etc.
      - Classes, workshops, etc.

Purpose: Show Otis that you will arrive with a diverse income and broader income skills

❑ Develop residual income streams that brings in at least $20 per month

- Must bring in at least $10 before this BB is complete from at least 2 different streams

❑ Perform some sort of labor over the internet and get paid at least $500

Do two of the following: (must include a tip of the hat to permaculture values)

❑ Sell "goods" (something you made, grew, upcycled or foraged) for a total of at least $200

❑ Sell your permaculture labor off-site for at least $500

❑ Get paid for an on-homestead service (cottage industry) for at least $500

Purpose: Show Otis that you will arrive with a substantial income and substantial income skills – all self-propelled

❑ Residual income minimum of $600 per month

- At least 4 different residual income streams

Then do one of these strategies :

❑ Strategy A – more residual income streams:

- Additional $600 per month
- At least 4 additional different streams

❑ Strategy B (Sepp Holzer lite) at least $5,000 from:

- On-site consultation or tours (people coming to experience all your hard work) (including on-site stays and meals)

❑ Strategy C: total $20,000. Includes on or off-site methods. Not a job. Must include a very strong correlation to permaculture values. Some examples:

- Raise and sell food
- Sell lumber cut from the land & milled on-site
- Nursery
- Sell goods
- Off-site permaculture labor
- Glamping
- Events
- Strategy B stuff
- Cottage industry stuff

113

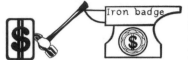

Purpose: Show that Otis's land will thrive financially under your care and/or to show you can financially carry a community – all self propelled

☐ Residual income minimum of $2,000 per month
  • At least 6 different reliable sources

Then do one of these strategies:
☐ Strategy A – huge residual income stream:
  • Additional $2,000 per month
  • At least 6 additional different reliable sources
☐ Strategy B (Sepp Holzer) at least $30,000 from:
  • On-site consultation or tours (people coming to experience all your hard work) (including on-site stays and meals)

Sample Sand Badge BB: Sell your permaculture labor off-site for at least $50

What is permaculture labor? For the purposes of this BB it's where you leave your property and do labor in exchange for money. Some examples:
• Creating earthworks
• Working in a permaculture garden
• Teaching a permaculture topic
• Doing a permaculture design
• Natural building
• Organizing a permaculture course
• Woodland care
• Cooking for a permaculture event
• Building a rocket mass heater (or rocket something)

Provide proof of the following as pictures or video (<2 mins):
  • A description of your labor and how it relates to permaculture
  • You doing the work
  • Proof that you got paid $50 or more (you can smudge out the personal info, so long as it is identifiable as you)

Clarification:
  • This could be several different activities/ sessions that add up to $50 or more

Sample Sand Badge BB: Start a cottage industry from your home

Show that you can make money from your home by providing a service for people. Must include a tip of the hat to permaculture values.

What is a Cottage Industry? For purposes of this BB it's where you do the work from your home, it's face to face and it's a service, not a transfer of goods.

Some examples:
  • Renting out a cabin, tent site, etc.
  • Sewing repair, truck repair, etc.
  • Massage, counseling, etc.
  • Classes, workshops, etc.

Provide proof of the following as pictures or video (<2 mins):
  • A description of your work and how it's a cottage industry
  • You doing the work
  • Proof that you got paid $50 or more (you can smudge out the personal info, so long as it is identifiable as you)

Clarification:
• This could be several different activities/sessions that add up to $50 or more

114

Sample Wood Badge BB:
Earn $5,000 from On-site
Consultations and/or On-Site Tours

For this BB, you will demonstrate you can make at least $5,000 from on-site consultations and on-site tours. You'll essentially be a permaculture Disneyland and try to make money by having people come to your place to experience the awesomeness of permaculture and to learn from you how to create and implement permaculture designs or techniques.

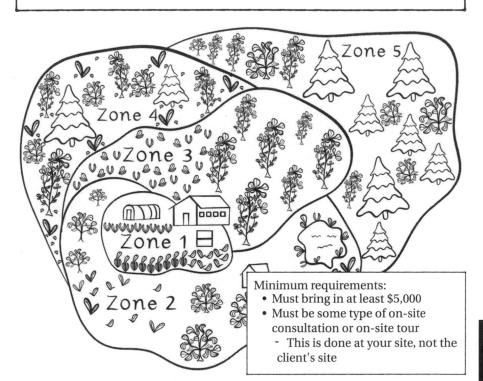

Minimum requirements:
- Must bring in at least $5,000
- Must be some type of on-site consultation or on-site tour
  - This is done at your site, not the client's site

Clarification:
- This could be several different activities/sessions that add up to $5,000 or more

Provide proof of the following as pictures or video (<2 mins):
- A description of the on-site consultations and/or on-site tours
- You doing the on-site consultations and/or on-site tours
- Proof that you got paid $5,000 or more (you can smudge out the personal info, so long as it is identifiable as you)

Chapter 31

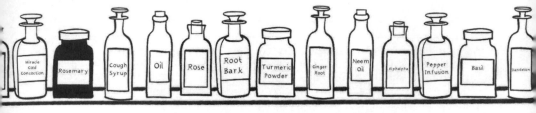

Natural Medicine

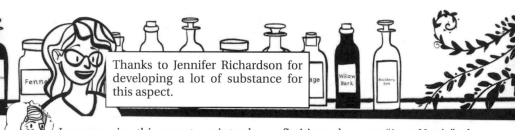

Thanks to Jennifer Richardson for developing a lot of substance for this aspect.

In composing this aspect, we introduce a fictitious character "Aunt Nattie" who:

- Has a rich stock of over-the-counter stuff (very natural)
- Is savvy to Google and has opinions on which information on the internet is stupid
- Will pick you up at the hospital and bring you home
- Will wait for you at the hospital when you get treatments
- Believes deeply in "food as medicine"
- Has a rich collection of simple herbal concoctions she has harvested and prepared herself
- Is ready to administer first aid
- Knows the best technique to pull out a tick
- Has a fresh salve for that scrape
- Sneaks greens into all of your food
- Has heard it all – no need to hold back
- Is passionate about your health

- Can give you a good idea of whether you should go to the doctor/hospital/naturopath
- Is a great cook
- Insists on organic or better
- Is keen on wildcrafting/foraging
- Has a huge permaculture garden – with lots of herbs
- Will make sure you do your physical therapy
- Will remind you to take your meds/vitamins/tea/whatever
- Keeps her house spic and span with cleaners you can eat
- Wants you to drink more water, go for a walk and get some sun
- Will slap that donut out of your pie hole

116

These badges are designed to put you on a track to developing the "Aunt Nattie" within you. You will start by building your collection of concoctions and then move into facing the challenges of ailments. As you apply your growing skills you might want to apply them to somebody. From here forward we will call that person your "friend."

The sand badge is to begin your collection of concoctions.

The straw badge is to complete your collection of concoctions, and begin to help people with ailments.

The wood badge is purely for helping people with their ailments and the iron badge is even more.

Starting with the straw badge we introduce two lists of ailments:

- The Quinn list is exclusively things for which you can get no more than half a point
- The Watson list is variable points – typically one or more points

There are some small things on the Quinn list for which half a point might seem a bit much. And there are some big things on the Quinn list that seem like they are on the wrong list. With the Watson list, we asked ourselves "What would be a metric we can take a picture of? Something that would prove improvement?" This level of documentation became the primary ingredient for the Watson list. Everything else had to remain on the Quinn list.

PEP

Natural Medicine

Featured Sand Badge BB: Make a fire cider vinegar infusion

Minimum requirements:
- Make at least one pint of fire cider

Provide proof of the following as pictures or video (<2 mins):
- Your ingredients being harvested (this should be more than half the ingredients)
- The ingredients you bought from the store (note, only buy the ingredients that do not grow local to your area – buying vinegar is fine)
- Your ingredients in vinegar
- Your completed fire cider in a labelled container

Sand badge

To receive a sand badge in natural medicine, complete one from each of the following sections:

Harvest, dry, and store one of the following for a tea, infusion, or decoction:

- Alfalfa leaf or blossom
- Blackberry leaf or root bark
- Burdock root
- Chamomile blossom
- Dandelion root

- Echinacea flower, leaf, or root
- Elderberries
- Fennel seed
- Ginger root
- Hibiscus blossom
- Hops

- Horsetail
- Lavender blossom
- Lemon balm
- Marshmallow root
- Mullein leaf
- Oat straw
- Oregano leaf

- ☐ Oregon grape stem or root bark
  - ☐ Parsley leaf
  - ☐ Peppermint leaf
  - ☐ Raspberry leaf
  - ☐ Red clover
- ☐ Rose hips, buds, blossom petals
- ☐ Rosemary
- ☐ Culinary sage leaf
- ☐ Slippery elm bark
- ☐ Stinging nettle leaf
- ☐ Strawberry leaf
- ☐ Thyme leaf
- ☐ Tulsi (holy basil) leaf
- ☐ Uva ursi (kinnikinnik)
- ☐ Willow bark

Create an infusion (hot or cold) of one of the following (fresh or dried):

- ☐ Alfalfa leaf or flower
- ☐ Blackberry leaves
- ☐ Chamomile blossom
- ☐ Dandelion leaves
- ☐ Echinacea flower or leaf
- ☐ Elderberry flowers or berries
- ☐ Fennel seeds
- ☐ Ginger root
- ☐ Hops flowers
- ☐ Horsetail
- ☐ Lavender blossom
- ☐ Lemon balm leaf
- ☐ Marshmallow root
- ☐ Mullein leaf or root
- ☐ Oatstraw
- ☐ Peppermint leaf
- ☐ Raspberry leaf
- ☐ Red clover blossom
- ☐ Rose hips, buds, or petals
- ☐ Rosemary leaf
- ☐ Slippery elm bark
- ☐ Stinging nettle leaf
- ☐ Strawberry leaf
- ☐ Thyme leaf
- ☐ Tulsi (holy basil) leaf
- ☐ Uva ursi (kinnikinnick) leaf

Create a decoction of one of the following (fresh or dried):

- ☐ Blackberry root bark
- ☐ Burdock root
- ☐ Dandelion root
- ☐ Echinacea root
- ☐ Garlic bulb
- ☐ Ginger root
- ☐ Mullein root
- ☐ Oregon grape stem bark or root bark
- ☐ Stinging nettle leaf
- ☐ Thyme
- ☐ Willow bark

Create a tincture of one of the following (fresh or dried):

- ☐ Blackberry root bark
- ☐ Burdock root or seed
- ☐ Calendula blossom
- ☐ Cayenne fruit
- ☐ Dandelion root
- ☐ Echinacea blossom, leaf or root
- ☐ Elderberry flowers or berries
- ☐ Ginger root
- ☐ Hops
- ☐ Mullein root, leaf, or blossom
- ☐ Oregano leaf
- ☐ Oregon grape stem or root bark
- ☐ Parsley
- ☐ Plantain leaf
- ☐ Rosemary
- ☐ Culinary sage
- ☐ St. John's wort blossoms
- ☐ Stinging nettle leaf
- ☐ Thyme tincture
- ☐ Uva ursi leaf
- ☐ Yarrow leaf or blossom
- ☐ Fennel seed

Create a vinegar infusion of one of the following (fresh or dried):

- ☐ Garlic
- ☐ Elderberry
- ☐ Fire cider
- ☐ Lavender blossom plus hibiscus blossom
- ☐ Lemon balm
- ☐ Parsley
- ☐ Rosemary leaf
- ☐ Culinary sage leaf
- ☐ Thyme

Create syrup or gummies from one of the following (fresh or dried):

- ☐ Blackberry
- ☐ Burdock
- ☐ Chamomile
- ☐ Fennel seed
- ☐ Echinacea blossom, leaf or root
- ☐ Elderberry
- ☐ Ginger root
- ☐ Rosehip
- ☐ Thyme

Create an oil infusion of one of the following (fresh or dried):

- ☐ Arnica blossom
- ☐ Balm of Gilead (cottonwood buds)
- ☐ Burdock root
- ☐ Calendula blossom
- ☐ Comfrey leaf
- ☐ Elderberry flower
- ☐ Ginger root
- ☐ Lavender blossom
- ☐ Marshmallow root
- ☐ Mullein blossom and garlic
- ☐ Mullein leaf
- ☐ Rose blossom
- ☐ Rosemary
- ☐ Peppermint leaf
- ☐ Plantain leaf
- ☐ St. John's wort blossom
- ☐ Stinging nettle
- ☐ Tulsi (holy basil) leaf
- ☐ Yarrow leaf or blossom

Create a salve from one of the following (fresh or dried):

- ☐ Arnica blossom
- ☐ Balm of Gilead (cottonwood buds)
- ☐ Burdock root
- ☐ Calendula blossom
- ☐ Chamomile
- ☐ Comfrey leaf
- ☐ Elderberry flower
- ☐ Ginger root
- ☐ Lavender blossom
- ☐ Marshmallow root
- ☐ Mullein leaf
- ☐ Rose blossom
- ☐ Rosemary
- ☐ Peppermint leaf
- ☐ Plantain leaf
- ☐ St. John's Wort blossom
- ☐ Stinging nettle
- ☐ Tulsi (holy basil) leaf
- ☐ Yarrow leaf or blossom

Create a poultice of one of the following (fresh or dried):

- ☐ Aloe leaf
- ☐ Arnica blossom
- ☐ Comfrey leaf
- ☐ Burdock root
- ☐ Calendula blossom
- ☐ Dandelion leaf or root
- ☐ Ginger root
- ☐ Mullein leaf
- ☐ Onion
- ☐ Plantain leaf
- ☐ Yarrow leaf or blossom

Complete 40 new BBs from the Sand badge
- At least 10 from the harvest, dry, and store herb list
- At least 3 from each of the 8 remaining categories (infusion, decoction, tincture, vinegar infusion, oil infusion, syrup/gummy, salve, poultice)

Straw badge

Complete 10 different BBs from the Quinn list
- At least 5 different times your concoctions were part of the solution

Quinn List:

Items on the Quinn List can't be proven with tests or photographic evidence. Some ailments that can be proven at times are sorted into Level 1 (not provable - Quinn List) and Level 2 (provable - Watson List (defined later)).

- ☐ Acid reflux/GERD
- ☐ Acne (level 1)
- ☐ Abrasion (level 1)
- ☐ Alzheimer's/dementia (level 1)
- ☐ Anxiety
- ☐ Arthritis/joint pain
- ☐ Bee/wasp/insect sting or bite
- ☐ Brain fog/difficulty concentrating
- ☐ Bruise
- ☐ Burn
- ☐ Cervical radiculopathy
- ☐ Cold/flu
- ☐ Colic
- ☐ Constipation
- ☐ COVID
- ☐ Cut
- ☐ Dandruff (level 1)
- ☐ Delayed onset muscle soreness (after working out or unaccustomed physical exertion)
- ☐ Depression
- ☐ Diarrhea
- ☐ Earache/ear infection
- ☐ Epilepsy/seizures

- ❑ Fatigue/low energy
- ❑ Foot fungus/athlete's foot (level 1)
- ❑ Gallstones
- ❑ Headache/migraine
- ❑ Head lice
- ❑ Inflammatory bowel disease (level 1)
- ❑ Inflammatory bowel syndrome
- ❑ Insomnia
- ❑ Kidney stones
- ❑ Menstrual cramps

- ❑ Morning sickness/ first-trimester sickness
- ❑ Motion sickness
- ❑ Muscle cramps
- ❑ Plantar fasciitis
- ❑ PMS
- ❑ Poison ivy/oak/ sumac/etc exposure
- ❑ Puncture wound
- ❑ Rash
- ❑ Repetitive stress injury/repetitive motion injury

- ❑ Seasonal allergies
- ❑ Sore/strained/pulled muscle
- ❑ Sore throat
- ❑ Sprain
- ❑ Stomach ulcer
- ❑ Sunburn
- ❑ Stomachache/ indigestion
- ❑ Toothache
- ❑ Urinary tract infection
- ❑ Vomiting

Wood badge

❑ Prove you helped at least 6 different people

Complete 180 points from the Quinn and Watson lists
- Including guided cancer care
- Quinn BBs count for ½ point
- Complete at least 25 different BBs
- Up to 30 points of duplication allowed
- At least 20 different times your concoctions were part of the solution

For "hosted care" provide an environment (clothing, bedding, shelter) with very low toxins and provide permaculture food and drink for your friend. Explain and show what is different about your hosted environment and food compared to your friend's home environment.

Watson list:
Everything on this list will require documentation that proves improvement, such as before and after photos, blood tests, or imaging results, depending on the ailment.

- ❑ Acne (level 2) - 1 point
- ❑ Abrasion (level 2) - 1 point
- ❑ Alzheimer's/dementia (guided) (level 2) - 2 or 6 points
- ❑ Alzheimer's/dementia (hosted) (level 2) - 50 points
- ❑ Bedsore - 3 points
- ❑ Cellulitis - 1 point
- ❑ Cancer care (guided) - 20 points
- ❑ Cancer care (hosted) - 200 points
- ❑ Chronic asthma - 2 points
- ❑ Chronic eczema/rosacea - 2 points
- ❑ Chronic/non-healing wound - 1-3 points

- ❑ Dandruff (level 2) - 1 point
- ❑ Diabetes (Type 1) - 3 points
- ❑ Diabetes (Type 2) (guided) - 3 points
- ❑ Diabetes (Type 2) (hosted) - 30 points
- ❑ Food allergies - 3 points

- Foot fungus/athlete's foot (level 2) - 1 point
- Fracture or broken bone rehab (guided) - 3 points
- Fracture or broken bone rehab (hosted) - 20 points
- Gout - 1 point
- Graves' disease (guided) - 3 points
- Graves' disease (hosted) - 20 points
- Hashimoto's thyroiditis (guided) - 3 points
- Hashimoto's thyroiditis (hosted) - 20 points
- High blood pressure - 1 point
- High blood sugar - 1 point
- High cholesterol - 1 point
- High triglycerides - 1 point
- Inflammatory bowel disease (level 2) - 2 points
- Iron-deficiency anemia - 1 point
- Iron overload disorder (excessive iron levels) - 1 point
- Low blood pressure - 1 point
- Obesity (guided) - 2 points
- Obesity (hosted) - 30 points
- Osteoporosis (guided) - 3 points
- Osteoporosis (hosted) - 30 points
- Paralysis rehab (guided) - 5 points
- Paralysis rehab (hosted) - 30 points
- Periodontitis - 1 point
- Pneumonia (guided) - 3 points
- Pneumonia (hosted) - 15 points
- Psoriasis (guided) - 1 point
- Psoriasis (hosted) - 12 points
- Rheumatoid arthritis - 2 points
- Ruptured/torn muscle, ligament, or tendon rehab (guided) - 5 points
- Ruptured/torn muscle, ligament, or tendon rehab (hosted) - 30 points
- Stroke rehab (guided) - 5 points
- Stroke rehab (hosted) - 30 points
- Toenail fungus - 2 points

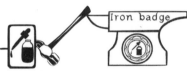

Iron badge

- Prove you helped at least 15 different people

Complete 1030 points from the Quinn and Watson lists
- Including hosted cancer care
- Quinn BBs count for ½ point
- Complete at least 60 different BBs (these can be repeats of BBs completed for prior badges)
- Unlimited duplication allowed

Sample Sand Badge BB:
Make a cayenne fruit tincture

PEP

Natural Medicine

Minimum requirements:
- Make 2 ounces of tincture
- Cayenne must be fully blended/mashed to ensure proper exposure to the alcohol
- At least 40% alcohol by volume

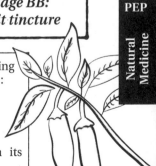

Provide proof of the following as pictures or video (<2 mins):
- The cayenne, either harvested by you or purchased
- The tincture being made
- The finished tincture in its labeled jar
- The recipe

Sample Straw Badge BB:
Help with a Urinary Tract Infection

Minimum requirements:
- Help your friend with their urinary tract infection problem
- Refer to them by a number or pseudonym that you will continue to use for that friend throughout the Natural Medicine badge

To document completion of the BB, provide the following:
- Your friend's pseudonym
- Describe the issue your friend is struggling with
  - Symptoms
  - Duration
  - Severity
  - Medical diagnosis (if any)
- Your suggestions for relief (including, but not limited to)
  - Behavioral
  - Food as medicine
  - Concoctions
- Description of success (including, but not limited to)
  - What your friend actually did
  - How well it worked
  - How long it took to see results
- Picture of you with your friend on the first meeting
- Picture of you with your friend (giving a thumbs up) on your last meeting

Chapter 32

Nest

Thanks to Nicole Alderman for developing a lot of substance for this aspect.

"I think the hard thing about Nest is that it is largely an ONGOING thing. If one does not keep doing the same, often-annoying, repetitive tasks, one does not have a good nest." ~ Nicole Alderman

You might think that everything in this list is simple and obvious. But experience has taught us that there are a lot of people who have never done most of these things. If you have done this before, all you need to do is take some pictures – no big deal.

This badge places a heavy emphasis on cleaning without toxic commercial cleaners.

Otis doesn't rent out his "old house" anymore because people didn't take care of it. Otis is thinking of offering you full run of that house but he needs to know that you will take good care of it.

Featured Sand Badge BB: Clean an oily dish without soap

Most soaps are toxic, but they do serve a powerful function. Soap is an emulsifier – making oils water soluble. Eliminating unwanted oils can be done without soap.

Provide proof of the following as pictures or video (<2 mins):
- The oily dish
- The food scraps going into a compost or animal bucket
- The plate being wiped with a piece of paper for future fire starter
- The last bit of oil being removed with hot water
- The newly clean dish

Minimum requirements:
- Clean an oily dish without soap
  - Not a skillet/pan/pot/etc.
  - Most goes into a compost or animal bucket
  - Much of the remainder can be wiped out with a piece of paper that will later be a fire starter
  - The last little bit is removed with hot water
  - End result is squeaky clean

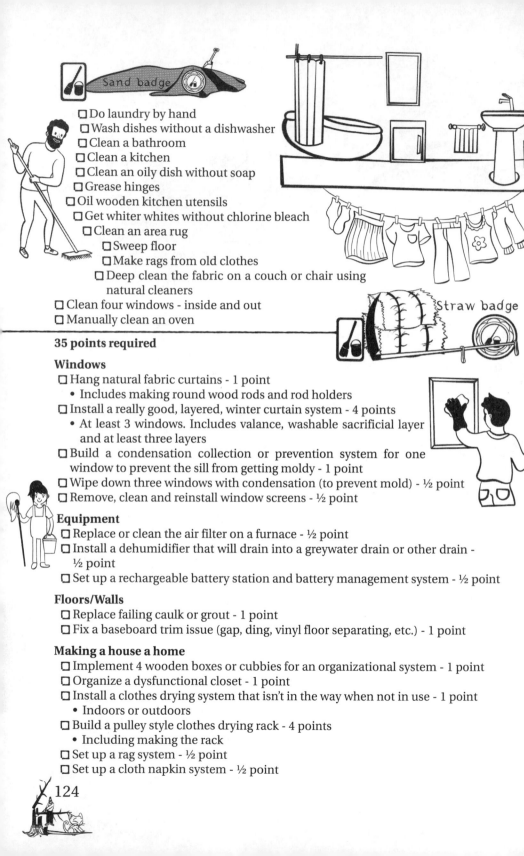

Sand badge

- ☐ Do laundry by hand
- ☐ Wash dishes without a dishwasher
- ☐ Clean a bathroom
- ☐ Clean a kitchen
- ☐ Clean an oily dish without soap
- ☐ Grease hinges
- ☐ Oil wooden kitchen utensils
- ☐ Get whiter whites without chlorine bleach
- ☐ Clean an area rug
  - ☐ Sweep floor
  - ☐ Make rags from old clothes
  - ☐ Deep clean the fabric on a couch or chair using natural cleaners
- ☐ Clean four windows - inside and out
- ☐ Manually clean an oven

Straw badge

35 points required

Windows

- ☐ Hang natural fabric curtains - 1 point
  - Includes making round wood rods and rod holders
- ☐ Install a really good, layered, winter curtain system - 4 points
  - At least 3 windows. Includes valance, washable sacrificial layer and at least three layers
- ☐ Build a condensation collection or prevention system for one window to prevent the sill from getting moldy - 1 point
- ☐ Wipe down three windows with condensation (to prevent mold) - ½ point
- ☐ Remove, clean and reinstall window screens - ½ point

Equipment

- ☐ Replace or clean the air filter on a furnace - ½ point
- ☐ Install a dehumidifier that will drain into a greywater drain or other drain - ½ point
- ☐ Set up a rechargeable battery station and battery management system - ½ point

Floors/Walls

- ☐ Replace failing caulk or grout - 1 point
- ☐ Fix a baseboard trim issue (gap, ding, vinyl floor separating, etc.) - 1 point

Making a house a home

- ☐ Implement 4 wooden boxes or cubbies for an organizational system - 1 point
- ☐ Organize a dysfunctional closet - 1 point
- ☐ Install a clothes drying system that isn't in the way when not in use - 1 point
  - Indoors or outdoors
- ☐ Build a pulley style clothes drying rack - 4 points
  - Including making the rack
- ☐ Set up a rag system - ½ point
- ☐ Set up a cloth napkin system - ½ point

124

☐ Set up a system for collecting burnables - ½ point
☐ Set up a system for dealing with wood ash - ½ point
☐ Set up a charcoal collection system - ½ point
☐ Set up a recycling system - ½ point
☐ Find a wall stud and hang a picture (first try with the nail hitting the stud) - ½ point
☐ Hang a picture or mirror level with two fasteners - ½ point
☐ Hang a shelf level - ½ point
☐ Repair ding in drywall or plaster - ½ point
☐ Install a medicine cabinet that goes in the wall between the studs - 2 points
☐ Make a moth or pest repellent sachet - ½ point
☐ Install coat hooks by a door to the outside - ½ point

Outside
☐ Clean exterior walls of house - 4 points
☐ Pressure wash a deck or hard surface to remove moss and gunk - 1 point
☐ Replace a locking door knob - ½ point
☐ Install a mailbox by the street - 1 point
☐ Install a permanent clothes line - 1 point
☐ Set up an elaborate clothes line - 1 point
☐ Shovel snow from a walk - ½ point
☐ Sand on ice - ½ point
☐ Install large enough house numbers for Emergency Responders to see - ½ point
☐ Set up a semi-permanent outside eating/gathering/relaxing area - ½ point
☐ Set up a big semi-permanent outside eating/gathering/relaxing area - 1 point
☐ Set up a huge semi-permanent outside eating/gathering/relaxing area - 2 points
☐ Set up a big permanent outside eating/gathering/relaxing area - 4 points
☐ Set up a huge permanent outside eating/gathering/relaxing area - 8 points
☐ Set up an outside classroom area - 2 points
   • Room for 10 students to face an instructor, chalk board or video screen and rain protected
☐ Set up a hygienic off-grid manual dishwashing station for parties or an event - 4 points
   • Includes 4 cleaning bins (pre, wash, rinse, sterilize), compost bucket, drying racks and dish storage

Cleaners/cleaning
☐ Remove mold from a place - ½ point
☐ Make a general purpose natural cleaner - ½ point
☐ Make a broom - 1 point
☐ Make a mop - 1 point
☐ Make a feather duster - ½ point
☐ Clean a set of curtains - 1 point
☐ Deep clean a couch with water and suction - 1 point
☐ Wash vehicle exterior - 1 point
☐ Clean vehicle interior - 1 point
☐ Clean a carpet with water (or steam) and suction - 1 point
☐ Remove a tough stain from carpet - ½ point
☐ Clean the grout in a shower or on a tile floor - 2 points

PEP Nest

□ Clean interior walls and ceilings of a room - 2 points
□ Deep clean the interior of a refrigerator - 1 point
□ Deep clean the interior of a freezer - 1 point
□ Deep clean the exterior of a refrigerator - 1 point
□ Deep clean the exterior of the washer and dryer - 1 point
□ Deep clean the exterior of the stove/oven - 1 point
□ Clean out the exhaust duct on a clothes dryer - ½ point
□ Run a self cleaning oven - ½ point
□ Run a "self clean" cycle in a washing machine (or manual option with vinegar) - ½ point
□ Remove knobs from shower or sink faucets to clean under - ½ point
□ Deep clean and polish a stainless steel sink - ½ point

 Wood badge There is no Wood or Iron badge at this time

Minimum requirements:
• Wash dishes without a dishwasher
  - Use minimal soap
    · Must be greywater friendly soap (the soap usually says "greywater safe" or "readily biodegradable")
• Fill a dishwasher with clean dishes using less than 3 gallons of water
  - Or approximate equivalent
    · Might require five rounds in a small dish rack
  - Yes, you are using the dishwasher as a dish drying rack

Sample Sand Badge BB: Wash dishes by hand

Provide proof of the following as pictures or video (<2 mins):
• Dirty dishes
• Progress of the dishes being washed
• The completed dishes with obviously less than 3 gallons water used
• Describe the soap used, its greywater friendliness, and a link to the verifiable biodegradable dish soap

Sample Sand Badge BB: Wash clothes by hand

Minimum requirements:
• Manual clothes washer, bathtub or large bucket
• Dry on a clothesline or drying rack
• At least "a standard load" (about eight large items and a bunch of socks and undies, etc.)

Provide proof of the following as pictures or video (<2 mins):
• Two points while clothes are being washed
• Clothes being dried
• Clothes folded

Sample Sand Badge BB: Oil kitchen woods

Minimum requirements:
• You must oil at least 6 wooden utensils, cutting boards, bowls, etc.
  - Walnut oil is best
  - If allergic to nuts, explain your oil choice
  - Oil must be edible and not made from petroleum

Provide proof of the following as pictures or video (<2 mins):
• Wooden items in need of oiling
• Action shot of you oiling one of the kitchen items
• All the wooden kitchen items you oiled
• Listing the type of oil you used. If other than walnut oil, please explain

126

Chapter 33

Homesteading

This aspect is a list of bits and bobs that don't fit into other aspects. Mostly:

- Conventional homestead techniques and projects
- Projects might involve glue, paint, and toxins that we typically want to minimize in the other aspects
- A few things that might fit better in another aspect, but that aspect was "full"

When you inherit the land from Otis, you will get two homes. The "old house" that Otis was born in and the "new house" that Otis built. Even if you build three new wofatis and most of the property is a permaculture heaven, these original buildings need to be properly cared for – and that care will require techniques and materials that fall outside our vision of permaculture. Prove to Otis that what he leaves to you will be well cared for. And prove to Otis what you are made of – on his terms.

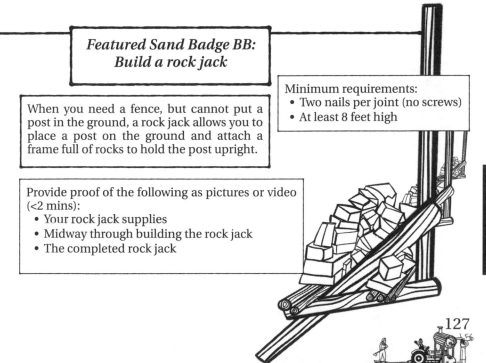

Featured Sand Badge BB: Build a rock jack

When you need a fence, but cannot put a post in the ground, a rock jack allows you to place a post on the ground and attach a frame full of rocks to hold the post upright.

Minimum requirements:
- Two nails per joint (no screws)
- At least 8 feet high

Provide proof of the following as pictures or video (<2 mins):
- Your rock jack supplies
- Midway through building the rock jack
- The completed rock jack

127

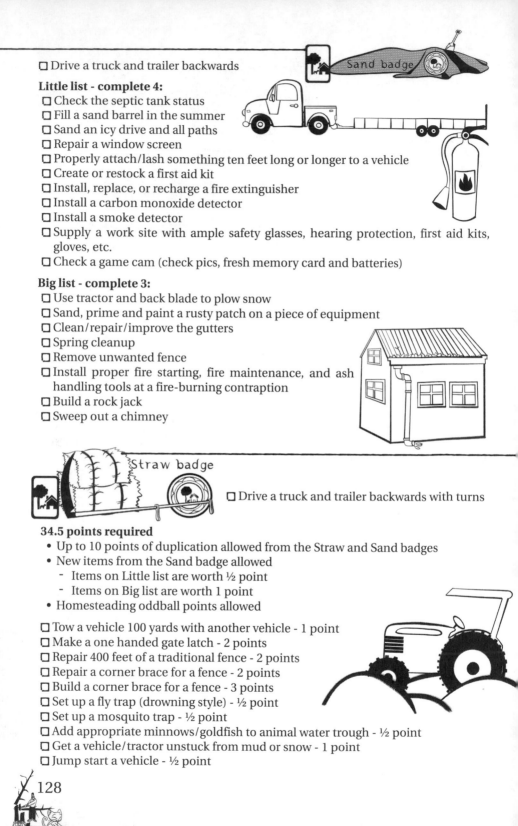

☐ Drive a truck and trailer backwards

Little list - complete 4:
☐ Check the septic tank status
☐ Fill a sand barrel in the summer
☐ Sand an icy drive and all paths
☐ Repair a window screen
☐ Properly attach/lash something ten feet long or longer to a vehicle
☐ Create or restock a first aid kit
☐ Install, replace, or recharge a fire extinguisher
☐ Install a carbon monoxide detector
☐ Install a smoke detector
☐ Supply a work site with ample safety glasses, hearing protection, first aid kits, gloves, etc.
☐ Check a game cam (check pics, fresh memory card and batteries)

Big list - complete 3:
☐ Use tractor and back blade to plow snow
☐ Sand, prime and paint a rusty patch on a piece of equipment
☐ Clean/repair/improve the gutters
☐ Spring cleanup
☐ Remove unwanted fence
☐ Install proper fire starting, fire maintenance, and ash handling tools at a fire-burning contraption
☐ Build a rock jack
☐ Sweep out a chimney

☐ Drive a truck and trailer backwards with turns

34.5 points required
- Up to 10 points of duplication allowed from the Straw and Sand badges
- New items from the Sand badge allowed
  - Items on Little list are worth ½ point
  - Items on Big list are worth 1 point
- Homesteading oddball points allowed

☐ Tow a vehicle 100 yards with another vehicle - 1 point
☐ Make a one handed gate latch - 2 points
☐ Repair 400 feet of a traditional fence - 2 points
☐ Repair a corner brace for a fence - 2 points
☐ Build a corner brace for a fence - 3 points
☐ Set up a fly trap (drowning style) - ½ point
☐ Set up a mosquito trap - ½ point
☐ Add appropriate minnows/goldfish to animal water trough - ½ point
☐ Get a vehicle/tractor unstuck from mud or snow - 1 point
☐ Jump start a vehicle - ½ point

- Put chains on a set of drive tires (tractor, vehicle, etc.) - 1 point
- Cover something with a tarp so that it stays dry for 6 months - ½ point
- Cover cargo with a tarp so it stays dry during transit - ½ point
- Set up an equipment file for owner's manuals and other equipment information - ½ point
- Set up a spare parts kit in the shop for a piece of equipment - ½ point
- Make, attach and fill a mobile tool kit for a piece of equipment (shear pins, wrench, etc.) - 1 point
- Make a "carry all" attachment for a tractor - 3 points
- Set up a family reference document that explains how each part of the homestead works for the other residents - 1 point
- Scythe an area of 100 square feet - ½ point
- Harvest four cubic yards of fertility from a domestic animal system - 1 point
- Use a 3 point hitch implement on a tractor and do work for 15 min - ½ point
- Remove snow from a roof safely - 2 points
- Spread manure/compost on a pasture - 1/2 point
- Dragging/moving a large down tree 100 feet for processing - 1 point
- Build a gate for vehicles - 4 points
- Clean up messes made by prior owners or trespassers - 2 points per cubic yard
- Set up a short term covered materials storage area for peeled logs, fence posts, metal parts, etc - 1 point
- Set up a materials storage area for things that don't need protection from the weather (gravel, sand, bricks, blocks, rocks, etc.) - 1 point
- Set up a hidden boneyard - 1 point
- Salvage building materials from a small building - 8 points
- Correct a structural defect with an outbuilding - 4-16 points
- Fix a leaking roof - 2 points
- Correctly make a roof penetration - 2 points
- Set up a security camera system - 2-4 points
- Whitewash or limewash a barn - 3 points
- Repoint 200 square feet of rubble foundation - 8 points
- Winterize the property in the fall - 4 points
- Paint a 200 square foot wall - 2 points
- Add a lean-to to an existing building - 16 points
- Replace roof on a small building (<400 square feet) - 8 points
- Make a small Jean Pain compost system (4+ cubic yards) - 8 points
- Set up a ham radio system (including tower) - 8 points
- Run communication cable/wire 40 feet to a new spot - 1 point

Wood badge

- Drive a truck/tractor/vehicle backwards with a wagon (front wheels of wagon turn with tongue)

179.5 points required
- Do at least 3 items from this Wood badge
- Up to 30 new points from the Straw badge allowed
- Up to 40 points of duplication from this Wood badge allowed
- Homesteading oddball points allowed

- ❏ Salvage building materials from a large down building - 16 points
- ❏ Salvage and raze a large building - 40-100 points
- ❏ Move an outbuilding (simple to no foundation) to a new site - 8 points
- ❏ Move an outbuilding (more involved foundation) to a new site - 16 points
- ❏ Replace roof on a large building (>400 square feet) - 20 points
- ❏ Remove a silo - 20 points
- ❏ Shovel snow and sand ice for a winter (>8 times) - 10 points
- ❏ Build a free standing shop or barn (>300 square feet) - 80 points
- ❏ Build a small Oehler style greenhouse (<100 square feet) - 80 points
- ❏ Build a large Oehler style greenhouse (>100 square feet) - 120 points
- ❏ Make a large Jean Pain compost system (10+ cubic yards) - 24 points
- ❏ Put a 3 season (unheated, uninsulated) addition onto a house - 16 points (existing roof), 60 points (new roof)
- ❏ Put a 4 season (insulated space, to code) addition onto a house (at least 150 square feet) - 120 points

Iron badge

No Iron badge at this time

Sample Sand Badge BB:
Sand an icy driveway and paths

Provide proof of the following as pictures or video (<2 mins):
- Icy driveway and paths before sanding
- Icy driveway and paths after sanding

Minimum requirements:
- You must sand at least 60 feet of icy driveway
- You must sand at least 60 feet of paths

Sample Sand Badge BB:
Lash something 10 feet or longer to a vehicle

Provide proof of the following as pictures or video (<2 mins):
- Before the cargo has been attached to your vehicle
- After the cargo has been attached to your vehicle
- Clarity on how it is attached
- Vehicle and cargo at a new location to demonstrate that the cargo was secure

Minimum requirements:
- You must attach something ten feet or longer to a vehicle
- It must be clearly secure enough to safely handle highway speeds

Sample Sand Badge BB:
Clean/repair/improve gutters

Minimum requirements:
- Clean/repair/improve the gutters
  - Make sure the gutters are in good repair and draining to a proper spot

Provide proof of the following as pictures or video (<2 mins):
- Gutters before
- Midway through cleaning/repairing/improving the gutters
- After cleaning/repairing/improving the gutters

130

There are no specific tasks for these badges. This aspect is for unpredictable projects or creative solutions that aren't covered by existing aspects. Maybe you're building a tiny home. Maybe the mailbox needs to be re-installed. Maybe a conventional floor needs a small mend. Maybe a conventional window is broken, or a chair needs to be repaired. These solutions might involve paint, glue, tape, cement or other materials typically frowned upon.

The points awarded are based on a number of factors. Regardless of how long it took you to do the task, the math starts with:

The "Pro Factor": This is the number of hours it would take an expert to accomplish the task, with all the tools and materials in hand, and a bit of luck. It is expected that the person submitting a BB for scoring might have put 3 hours in and the evaluator will say that an expert would have completed that task in 15 minutes, therefore 0.25 points. From there the score is further adjusted by:

The "Piano Factor": This is an adjustment based upon how useful the project is to Otis. 1000 hours of piano construction is worth less to Otis than 1000 hours spent building a barn.

The "PEX Factor": This is an adjustment based on how closely the project aligns to X's permaculture values. For PEP it's Paul's values. Projects could be awarded extra points if they're particularly elegant solutions using permaculture principles. Generally though it's a way to discourage use of man-made materials and toxic gick.

As you progress through the levels of Oddball, the scoring shifts to put more emphasis on the PEX factor. So a good Otis-worthy project using conventional paint and caulk that takes you 16 hours may be awarded 4 points if you're at the Sand level, 2 points in Straw, 1 point in Wood or ½ point in Iron (this is just an example, not a formula).

Bonus! Any valid task that has a photo put up on Permies.com for evaluation, that an expert would have spent at least 7 minutes accomplishing, and that passes the PEX factor, will earn a minimum of a half point. Awarded points will be rounded up to the nearest half point. So for a task that the evaluator would award 45 minutes, rather than granting 0.75 points, the evaluator will grant 1 point.

Note: If your project will take a while to complete, don't post partial chunks over time in the thread. Start a thread elsewhere on the forums to document the project and then post a summary in the oddball thread.

PEP

Oddball

The Sand badge is granted for a score of 5.

This badge is designed to be more challenging to acquire than any other Sand badge.

The Straw badge is granted for a total score of 40 (including points from the Sand badge).

This badge is designed to be more challenging to acquire than any other Straw badge.

The Wood badge is granted for a total score of 220 (including points from the Sand and Straw badges).

This badge is designed to be more challenging to acquire than any other Wood badge.

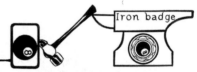

The Iron badge is granted for a total score of 1250 (including points from the Sand, Straw and Wood badges).

This badge is designed to be more challenging to acquire than any other Iron badge.

Step 1

Fold the left page
following the guide

Step 2

Move the folded page
on top of the right page

Step 3

PEA Gardening

Use organic (or better) permaculture techniques to grow nutritious food and improve air quality regardless of potential limitations in your location. Projects include fertilization methods, seed saving, and urban-friendly means of expanding your permaculture influence.

Sand badge

☐ Create a large potted polyculture (minimum 5 plants and 3 species)
☐ Grow a new plant from a cutting
☐ Grow a tray of micro-greens
☐ Sprout seeds for cooking
  ☐ Grow a table herb garden from seeds
    (Must include at least 4 herbs)
☐ Grow a tuber
  ☐ Grow a vegetable protein
  ☐ Grow a fruit
☐ Grow a vegetable
  ☐ Grow a grain
  ☐ Pot and maintain 2 plants inside your home to improve air quality

Do 5 of the following:
☐ Seed saving (may be from store bought fruits)
☐ Grow a plant from seeds you've saved
☐ Make a vermicompost tea (preferred) or compost tea (from homemade compost) and use it on your container(s)
☐ Create an indoor mushroom growing system from an existing household material such as spent coffee grounds
☐ Harvest a half pound of mushrooms from an indoor growing system
☐ Use vermicompost to fertilize indoor plants
☐ Use spent coffee grounds or other waste materials to fertilize indoor plants
☐ Set up a hanging plant
☐ Pot and maintain some other species of houseplant

Chapter 36

PEA Roundwood Woodworking

The PEA version of round wood woodworking is similar to the PEP version. It is still about using unprocessed wood to create new things without glue and largely without metal. As with the PEP aspect, power tools are generally discouraged. Many projects are about the joy of working with green wood, which is much easier to shape than dry wood. Unlike the PEP aspect, almost every project at the sand badge level is something small. The assumption is that space will be at a premium.

If you need to find sources of green wood, you can find permies offering solutions in the badge thread on Permies.com.

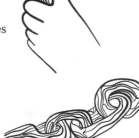

☐ Carve a sauerkraut stomper from a single piece of wood suitable for a wide-mouth jar using only hand tools

☐ Make a small compound mallet with hand tools only (green wood head, dry handle)

☐ Carve a simple beginner spoon with hand tools

Do 5 points worth of the following:
☐ Any PEP Roundwood task done to the PEP standard - 1 point
☐ Carve a dough bowl - 1 point (2 if done with only hand tools)
☐ Craft two coat hooks made from the branches of small trees (no joinery) - ½ point
☐ Craft a coat rack using dry pegs in green wood - 1 point
☐ Carve a letter opener - ½ point
☐ Carve a functional whistle - ½ point
☐ Carve a very basic chess set - 1.5 points
☐ Carve interesting coasters from 6 wooden disks - 1 point
☐ Carve a simple wood spirit - ½ point
☐ Carve a chain from a single piece of wood - 1 point
☐ Carve a ball in a cage from a single piece of wood - 1 point
☐ Carve a basic spatula with hand tools - ½ point
☐ Craft a simple cutting board or serving tray using hand tools - 1 point
☐ Ebonize a wooden object that you have carved - ½ point

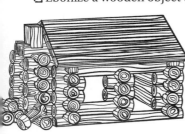

☐ Add faceting to another project - ½ point
☐ Create 24 homemade "Lucky Logs" (your own personal spin-off of a branded tiny log toy construction thing) with saddle notches using hand tools only - 1.5 point

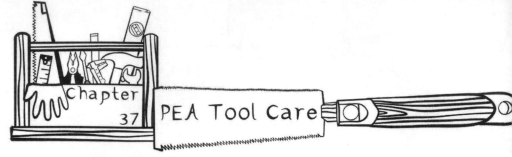

Chapter 37

PEA Tool Care

Every home has some tools. And a person pursuing PEA1 will need even more tools than that! Prove to Otis that you know how to keep your tools sharp, clean and well cared for.

Sand badge

☐ Sharpen three knives
☐ Sharpen a hand saw
☐ Sharpen scissors
☐ Sharpen a chisel
☐ Remove rust from and then oil a hand tool
☐ Sharpen a serrated blade with a round file
☐ Repair a kitchen appliance

Chapter 38

PEA Dimensional Lumber Woodworking

This aspect expects the same non-toxic approaches as the PEP aspect such as limited glue, no plywood or particle board, etc. All these projects can be completed with a few hand tools and they prepare you nicely for doing larger projects in the future.

As we created these projects we thought about the need for some people to be relatively quiet. So probably no hammering – although there are some hammering techniques that make very little sound. Screws would be best done with pilot holes – which would require drilling. And there are ways to drill a hole quietly.

Sand badge

☐ Wood-burned artwork
  • Installation isn't required

Complete 3 of the following (at least one of these projects features a dovetail joint):
  • Any PEP Dimensional Lumber BB done to the PEP standard
    - A few possibilities to consider:
        ☐ 2 step stool
        ☐ Wood box/crate
        ☐ Toolbox
        ☐ Shelf
  ☐ Basic birdhouse
    • Installation isn't required
  ☐ Cookbook holder
  ☐ Haybox cooker
  ☐ Bread box
  ☐ Vermiculture bin to process kitchen scraps
  ☐ Small bookshelf

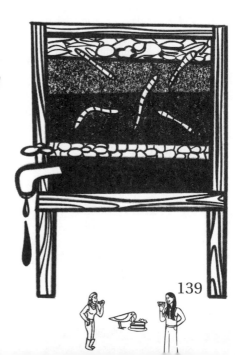

Most of the PEP sand badge works in an apartment, except for the rocket and solar bits... So we adjusted the list and added a few more BBs to compensate.

In other words, by completing this badge, you are about 70% of the way to completing the PEP sand badge and have a bit of a dent in the straw badge too!

Just like in PEP, the following are strictly forbidden:
- Aluminum cookware
- "Non-stick" coatings and similar materials
- Microwave ovens
- Plastic touching the food, including cooking utensils and storage bags

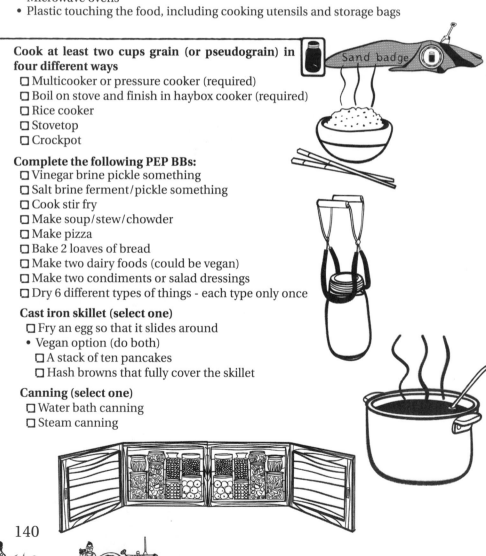

Cook at least two cups grain (or pseudograin) in four different ways
- ☐ Multicooker or pressure cooker (required)
- ☐ Boil on stove and finish in haybox cooker (required)
- ☐ Rice cooker
- ☐ Stovetop
- ☐ Crockpot

Complete the following PEP BBs:
- ☐ Vinegar brine pickle something
- ☐ Salt brine ferment/pickle something
- ☐ Cook stir fry
- ☐ Make soup/stew/chowder
- ☐ Make pizza
- ☐ Bake 2 loaves of bread
- ☐ Make two dairy foods (could be vegan)
- ☐ Make two condiments or salad dressings
- ☐ Dry 6 different types of things - each type only once

Cast iron skillet (select one)
- ☐ Fry an egg so that it slides around
- Vegan option (do both)
  - ☐ A stack of ten pancakes
  - ☐ Hash browns that fully cover the skillet

Canning (select one)
- ☐ Water bath canning
- ☐ Steam canning

Chapter 40

PEA Animal Care

silk worms

Worm bin

The limitations of an apartment can make animal care beyond a pet seem intimidating. Animal production in such spaces feels out of reach to many. However, it is entirely possible to encourage wildlife as well as to create productive animal systems in the confines of an apartment. Eggs, meat, fiber, compost, and natural pest control can all be accomplished in an apartment. We understand that this badge could work for most vegans but not all.

PEA

Food Prep & Preservation

PEA

Animal Care

Complete seven points:
Any PEP Animal Care BB done to the
PEP standard - 1 point (limit 5)

Sand badge

- A few possibilities to consider:
  - ☐ Live mouse trap
  - ☐ 6 toad habitats
  - ☐ Snake/lizard habitat
  - ☐ Collect 12 eggs
  - ☐ Food/water/safety check for your critters
  - ☐ Prove your animal's food is fit for human consumption
  - ☐ Breed a quail/guinea pig/rabbit/pigeon
  - ☐ Raise mealworms

☐ Build a nice birdhouse for a specific species of bird - 1 point
☐ Build a mason bee house (possibly other solitary bees) - ½ point
☐ Make a bee/insect watering station - ½ point
  ☐ Build a ladybug house - ½ point
  ☐ Build a bat house - 1 point
  ☐ Build an insect hotel - ½ point
  ☐ Create a vermicomposting system - 3 points
  ☐ Set up a black soldier fly larvae composting system - 1 point
  ☐ Raise silkworms to the cocoon stage - 1 point
  ☐ Mitigate a cockroach issue - ½ point
  ☐ Mitigate a bed bug issue - ½ point
  ☐ Mitigate a flea issue - ½ point
  ☐ Mitigate an ant issue - ½ point
☐ Mitigate a rodent issue - ½ point

141

Items that can be done in most apartments but not necessarily all apartments:

☐ Create a wild bird window feeder - ½ point
☐ Set up a freshwater aquarium - 2 points
  • At least 2 species of fish, 1 crab, 1 snail and 1 plant

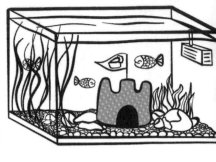

☐ Set up a saltwater aquarium - 2 points
  • At least 2 species of fish and 1 crab
☐ Share appropriate kitchen scraps with a vertebrate animal system - ½ point
  • Multiple times, 1 gallon in total
☐ Set up a home quail system - 2 points
  • Food, water, nest box, cage, bedding and multiple quail
☐ Set up a home rabbit enclosure - 2 points
  • Food, water, nesting area, cage, bedding and multiple rabbits

☐ Set up a home guinea pig enclosure - 2 points
  • Food, water, nesting area, cage, bedding and multiple guinea pigs
☐ Set up a pigeon system - 2 points
  • Food, water, nesting area, cage, bedding and multiple pigeons
☐ Feed the manure/bedding of an animal system into a vermicompost/black soldier fly system - ½ point

Chapter 41

PEA Foraging

I'm sure the first question you have is how in the world does one practice foraging without leaving an apartment?! 65% of foraging is becoming familiar with what the plant looks like and how to use it. This badge permits the purchase of the plant and focuses on preparing and eating it.

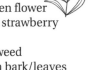

☐ Make 6 cups of tea
- Each from a different species
- Must be something that is commonly foraged (not something that is rarely foraged)
- There must be at least one sample of each species that is clearly identifiable
  - This could require more than one purchase/acquisition
- Can be a twofer with PEP Foraging BBs
- Species can be fresh or dried
  - Sassafrass
  - Spice bush
  - Wild ginger
  - Nettle
  - Rose hips
  - Mint
  - Pineapple weed
  - Raspberry leaves

  - Chaga mushrooms
  - Pine needle
  - Fir tip
  - Ceanothus americanus/New Jersey tea
  - Kinnikinnick
  - Sumac

  - Linden flower
  - Wild strawberry leaf
  - Fireweed
  - Birch bark/leaves
  - Clover
  - Rose petals
  - Dandelion
  - Bull thistle

☐ Prepare 6 dishes
- Each from a different category (below)
- One cup minimum per dish
- Must be something that is commonly foraged (not something that is rarely foraged)
- There must be at least one sample of each species that is clearly identifiable
  - This could require more than one purchase/acquisition
- Can be a twofer with PEP Foraging BBs

- Categories:
  - **Mushrooms**
    - Chanterelles
    - Puffballs
    - Oyster
    - Hen of the woods

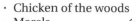
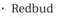

    - Chicken of the woods
    - Morels
    - Boletes

  - **Wildflowers**
    - Violet
    - Rose
    - Chickory
    - Dandelion

    - Redbud
    - Clover
    - Daylily

  - **Leafy greens/moss**
    - Reindeer moss
    - Dandelion
    - Plantain
    - Miner's lettuce

    - Purslane
    - Clover
    - Curly dock
    - Pigweed

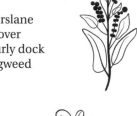

  - **Plant stems/shoots**
    - Purslane
    - Cattail
    - Asparagus (must be foraged)

  - **Starchy roots/tubers**
    - Dandelion
    - Burdock
    - Chickory root
    - Wild potato (must be foraged)

    - Ground nut
    - Cattail
    - Daylily

  - **Fruits/berries**
    - Bramble berries (raspberry, blackberry, etc) (must be foraged)
    - Wild plum (must be foraged)
    - Wild persimmon
    - Wild cherry (must be foraged)
    - Wild strawberry (must be foraged)

    - Lowbush blueberry (must be foraged)
    - Wild cranberry (must be foraged)
    - Serviceberry
    - Huckleberry
    - Banana (must be foraged)

  - **Grains/nuts**
    - Pigweed
    - Black walnut
    - Acorns
    - Hazelnuts
    - Hickory

    - Chestnuts
    - Pecans
    - Brazil nuts
    - Macadamia
    - Wild rice

  - **Bulbs**
    - Wild onion (must be foraged)
    - Wild garlic (must be foraged)
    - Camas

☐ Craft 6 pounds of seed balls
- At least an inch in diameter
- Quickly dry for storage (before the seeds germinate)
- At least six different species in each ball
  - Possible species:

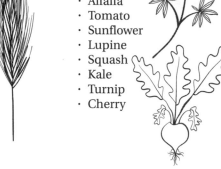

    · Nettle
    · Dandelion
    · Maple
    · Mulberry
    · Apples
    · Black locust
    · Sepp Holzer grain
    · Daikon radish

    · Alfalfa
    · Tomato
    · Sunflower
    · Lupine
    · Squash
    · Kale
    · Turnip
    · Cherry

Chapter 42
PEA Community Living

90% of all the challenges in permaculture are with community. The challenges of greening a desert pale in comparison to "20 people living under one roof without stabbing each other."

For the sake of this aspect, the word "community" refers to the goal of people sharing a home or homestead. We worked on creating BBs that focus on "building community" rather than "experiencing community." So while some of these skills could accidentally build a neighborhood community, the real focus is on the ability to re-apply these skills later to build a shared community.

The entire PEA program strives to limit the BBs to projects that could be done in a small apartment that has a lot of restrictions. We debated whether to offer this badge because it would require finding people and bringing them together. In the end, we decided to create it because:

- Most people pursuing PEA instead of PEP would be in a city or town.
- People pursuing PEA1 may opt out of 4 badges. For some people this will be their easiest badge while others may opt out of this one.
- Community is the most challenging aspect of permaculture and the most beneficial when done well. We want people to develop these skills early and often.

Do 4 of the following:
- Any PEP Community BB done to the PEP standard
- ☐ Host a gathering where at least 8 individuals attend
  - This BB can be done up to 3 times, as long as the type of events are different
  - Book club
  - Christmas party
  - Pizza feed
  - Potluck
  - Etc.
- ☐ Create physical artwork to be displayed in a public location
  - At least 1.5 hours of work
  - Can be installed later for a PEP BB

☐ Prepare something at home for a bake sale, auction, or other community event
☐ Get a roommate
- Prove the person moved in
- Describe how you found that person and why you think they'll be a good fit
- Not a family member

☐ Have a roommate for 8 months
- Assigned dorms, spouses and "shacking up" counts
- Needs to be the same person for the whole 8 months
- Not a family member

One of the following:
☐ A Youtube/Vimeo/Storyfire/Bitchute/etc. channel with at least 4 videos focused on aspects of permaculture or homesteading
- More than 100 views each

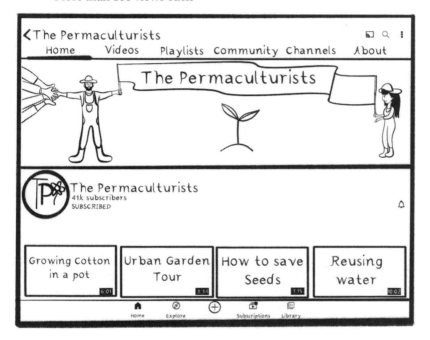

☐ A Blog/website about permaculture or homesteading topics
- At least 10 entries and 1000 pageviews total
☐ Create an engaging and informative Permies.com post
- At least 100 replies

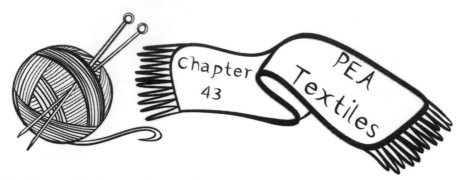

Chapter 43

PEA Textiles

The PEP sand badge is made entirely of projects that can be done in any apartment. So the PEA badge is to complete the PEP sand badge plus a bit more. Just like in PEP, synthetic materials are not allowed – even if they are recycled or repurposed.

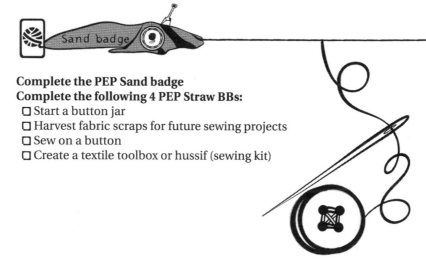

Sand badge

Complete the PEP Sand badge
Complete the following 4 PEP Straw BBs:
- ☐ Start a button jar
- ☐ Harvest fabric scraps for future sewing projects
- ☐ Sew on a button
- ☐ Create a textile toolbox or hussif (sewing kit)

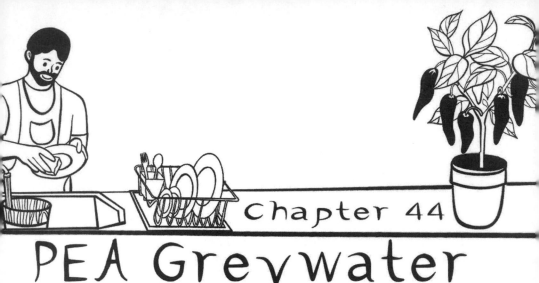

Chapter 44

PEA Greywater

Setting up a full willow feeder isn't possible for those living on a small property, in an apartment, or as part of a strongly regulated neighborhood. Even so, there are other ways for one to expand their skills and take action when it comes to working with greywater.

Sand badge

Do eight of the following:

☐ Use a bucket of water from a shower
☐ Use water from a dishpan
☐ Use water from cooking pasta/food
☐ Install a water recycler (for washing hands) on a toilet tank
☐ Make signage with laminated paper or sealed shelf paper
  • About water collection in the shower and the kitchen sink
  • About using collected water at the flush toilet
☐ Make signage (wood burned)
  • About water collection at the shower and the kitchen sink
  • About using collected water at the flush toilet
☐ Prove the value of a Berkey-style water filter
☐ Shower with non-chlorinated water
☐ Prove that you can wash dishes, by hand, in a way that uses less water than a dishwasher
☐ Thoroughly document water savings by going poo-less
  • Time 5 poo-less showers and compare to national average shower time
☐ Make a water filter (like a Berkey)

PLEASE
Use shower bucket
to flush the toilet.
Thank you!

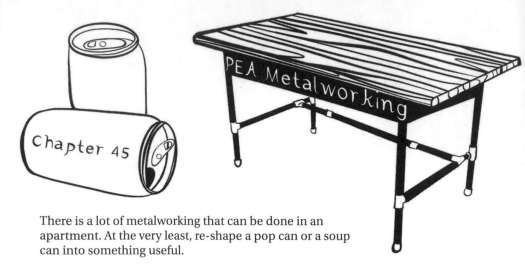

There is a lot of metalworking that can be done in an apartment. At the very least, re-shape a pop can or a soup can into something useful.

The PEA version of metalworking is focused heavily on working with sheet metal, filing, sandpaper, and small solder tasks. It makes use of pop, soup, and coffee cans, as well as sheet metal, wires, and other purchased materials. Just because blacksmithing or welding are off the table, doesn't mean you can't improve your metalworking repertoire.

- ☐ 6 "pop can" plant labels
  - Metal wire (or coat hanger) post
  - Aluminum pop can label embossed with ball point pen

- ☐ 6 sturdier garden or plant labels
  - The "post" must be metal and hold the "message" at least four inches off the soil
  - The "message" does not move in the wind
  - The wording must be able to last at least ten years outside
  - Possibilities include:
    - An old spoon, flattened and metal stamped
    - A piece of copper tube with one end flattened and legibly engraved
    - Cast aluminum with legibly chiseled letters
    - Denting metal with a ballpoint pen
    - Words made with a second layer of metal (e.g., gold leaf or solder)
    - Jeweler's saw to cut out the letters

5 points required
☐ Any PEP Metalworking BB done to the PEP standard
- A few possibilities to consider:
  - ☐ Build a kindling cracker - 4.5 points
  - ☐ Rocket mass heater scoop - ½ point
  - ☐ Dress up a mushroomed chisel or splitting wedge - ½ point
  - ☐ Copper flower - 1 point

Metal shaping projects
☐ Turn a box end wrench into a spoon carving knife - 2 points
☐ Key fob - ½ point
  • From a steel washer, old flatware handle or some piece of scrap metal
  • Must be stamped with a descriptor
☐ 6 coat/tool hangers from old flatware - ½ point
☐ 4 cabinet door knobs from railroad spikes - 1.5 points
  • With a tapped hole to accept a machine screw
☐ Dish draining tray out of a cookie sheet - ½ point
  • Sloped, drains into sink

Solder/brazing projects:
☐ Square/rectangle trivet from pipe - ½ point
☐ Towel bar - ½ point
  • Wall mount or freestanding
  • Could be for bath towel, hand towel, toilet paper, paper towel, etc.
☐ Boot drying rack - 1 point
  • Wall mount or freestanding
☐ Shoe rack - 1 point
☐ Small table - 1 point
  • Wood top, pipe for legs with soldered cross braces
☐ Pot/pan hanger - 1 point
  • Wall/ceiling mount or freestanding

Pop can projects:
☐ Pop can alcohol stove - ½ point
  • Show it can cook something
☐ Candle reflector - 1 point
  • Includes handle to carry burning candle
  • Show a little bit of polish on the reflecting surface
  • Open top to let light go up and avoid sooting up
☐ Cell phone holder - ½ point
☐ 6 cookie cutter shapes - ½ point

☐ Small box with fitted lid - 1 point
  • Square or rectangular
☐ Small box with a hinged lid - 1 point
  • Square or rectangular
☐ Open top tray with separations to hold loose screws and nuts - 2 points
  • At least four 2x2x2 inch compartments
  • Probably ample use of pop rivets
☐ Mirror - ½ point
☐ Pop can safe - ½ point
☐ Make 50 pieces of flat aluminum from cans (3 inches by 8 inches) - 1.5 points
  • Could someday be tiles for a "pop can roof" or a bird house

Wire coat hanger (or thick wire) projects:
☐ Slingshot - ½ point
☐ Conifer Christmas wreath - ½ point
☐ Houseplant trellis - ½ point
☐ 6 key rings - ½ point
☐ Giant safety pin or carabiner - ½ point

☐ Drain cleaner - ½ point
☐ Chip clip - ½ point
☐ Rope making jig - 2 points
☐ Big sewing needle - ½ point

Most landlords dislike major changes to their properties by the renter. Therefore the experiences in this badge focus on things you can do without upsetting a concerned landlord.

Complete 6 points

- ☐ Any PEP Electricity BB done to the PEP standard
  - A few possibilities to consider:
    - ☐ Create a micro heater bubble - 1 point
    - ☐ Replacing a bathroom fan switch with a timer - ½ point
    - ☐ Repair a light switch - ½ point
    - ☐ Install a permanent light fixture - ½ point
    - ☐ Put a new end on an extension cord - ½ point
    - ☐ Repair a lamp - ½ point
    - ☐ Label the breakers on an electrical panel - ½ point
    - ☐ Set up an emergency back-up battery system that is always charged - 1 point
    - ☐ Document electrical usage of 12 devices with a Kill-A-Watt - 2 points
- ☐ Craft a miniaturized solar water pump - 1 point
  - Light shines on solar panel and water pumps
- ☐ Craft a small and portable DC only solar system - 2.5 points
  - Minimum of 200 watt-hours
- ☐ Build a lamp - 1 point

Chapter 47

PEA
Commerce

This is a badge focused on increasing your experience with multiple forms of obtaining an income that is sustainable and aligned with permaculture principles. By developing income streams in advance of owning a homestead, you are dedicating energy now to sustain your activities later. A strong showing in this badge will indicate you arrive with an existing income and that you are dedicated to earning money through your permaculture efforts. The idea is that you can remain on the land inherited from an Otis working to improve it rather than having to spend 40 or more hours a week away. It stands as proof that you will use what you inherit rather than cashing it out.

Sand badge

☐ Develop a possible residual income stream that brings in at least $10 per year
☐ Perform some sort of labor over the internet and get paid at least $60

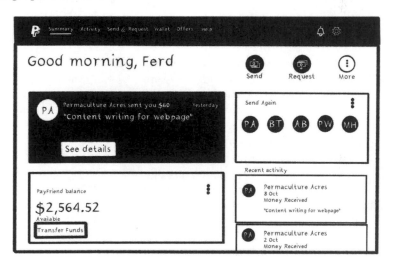

Do 2 of the following tasks (must include clear permaculture values)
☐ Sell "goods" grown, composed or crafted from natural materials for a total of at least $25
☐ Sell "goods" you have made from upcycled materials for at least $25
☐ Get paid for in-home services (cottage industry) for at least $60

PEA

Electricity

PEA

Commerce

153

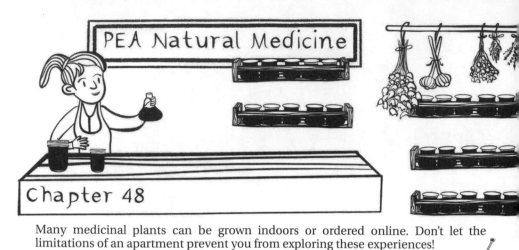

PEA Natural Medicine

Chapter 48

Many medicinal plants can be grown indoors or ordered online. Don't let the limitations of an apartment prevent you from exploring these experiences!

Complete 12 unique BBs from those below, including at least 1 from each of the sections:

(Note: Any Sand PEP BB done to the PEP standard counts here as well)

Acquire fresh (probably purchase), dry, and store enough for a tea, infusion or decoction

- ☐ Burdock root
- ☐ Dandelion root
- ☐ Ginger root
- ☐ Licorice root
- ☐ Oregano
- ☐ Parsley
- ☐ Peppermint leaf
- ☐ Rosemary
- ☐ Culinary sage
- ☐ Thyme
- ☐ Tulsi

Create a vinegar infusion with fresh or dried ingredients

- ☐ Elderberry
- ☐ Fire cider
- ☐ Garlic
- ☐ Lavender blossom plus hibiscus blossom
- ☐ Lemon balm
- ☐ Parsley
- ☐ Rosemary leaf
- ☐ Culinary sage leaf
- ☐ Thyme

Create an oil infusion from fresh or dried materials

- ☐ Arnica blossom
- ☐ Balm of Gilead (cottonwood buds)
- ☐ Burdock root
- ☐ Calendula blossom
- ☐ Comfrey leaf
- ☐ Elderberry flower
- ☐ Ginger root
- ☐ Lavender blossom
- ☐ Marshmallow root
- ☐ Mullein blossom and garlic
- ☐ Mullein leaf
- ☐ Rose blossom
- ☐ Rosemary
- ☐ Peppermint leaf
- ☐ Plantain leaf
- ☐ Stinging nettle
- ☐ Tulsi
- ☐ Yarrow blossom

Create a salve from fresh or dried materials

- ☐ Arnica blossom
- ☐ Balm of Gilead (cottonwood buds)
- ☐ Burdock root
- ☐ Calendula blossom
- ☐ Chamomile
- ☐ Comfrey leaf
- ☐ Elderberry flower
- ☐ Ginger root
- ☐ Lavender blossom
- ☐ Marshmallow root
- ☐ Mullein leaf
- ☐ Rose blossom
- ☐ Rosemary
- ☐ Peppermint leaf
- ☐ Plantain leaf
- ☐ Stinging nettle
- ☐ Tulsi
- ☐ Yarrow blossom

Create a tincture from fresh or dried materials

- Blackberry root bark
- Burdock root or seed
- Calendula blossom
- Cayenne fruit
- Dandelion root
- Echinacea blossom, leaf or root
- Elderberry flower or berries

- Fennel seed
- Ginger root
- Hops
- Mullein root, leaf, or blossom
- Oregano leaf
- Oregon grape stem or root bark
- Parsley

- Plantain leaf
- Rosemary
- Culinary sage
- Stinging nettle leaf
- Thyme
- Uva ursi leaf
- Yarrow

Create a poultice from fresh or dried materials

- Aloe leaf
- Arnica blossom
- Comfrey leaf
- Burdock root
- Calendula blossom

- Dandelion leaf or root
- Ginger root
- Mullein leaf
- Onion

- Plantain leaf
- Yarrow blossom or leaf

Create a syrup or gummies from fresh or dried materials

- Blackberry
- Burdock
- Chamomile

- Echinacea blossom, leaf or root
- Elderberry
- Fennel seed

- Ginger root
- Rose hip
- Thyme

Create an infusion/tea (hot or cold) from fresh or dried materials

- Alfalfa leaf or flower
- Blackberry leaves
- Chamomile blossom
- Dandelion leaves
- Echinacea flower or leaf
- Elderberry flowers or berries
- Fennel seeds
- Ginger root

- Hops flowers
- Horsetail
- Lavender blossom
- Lemon balm leaf
- Marshmallow root
- Mullein leaf or root
- Oatstraw
- Peppermint leaf
- Raspberry leaf
- Red clover blossom

- Rose hips, buds, or petals
- Rosemary leaf
- Slippery elm bark
- Stinging nettle leaf
- Strawberry leaf
- Thyme leaf
- Tulsi (holy basil) leaf
- Uva ursi (kinnikinnick) leaf

Create a decoction from fresh or dried materials

- Blackberry root bark
- Burdock root
- Dandelion root
- Echinacea root
- Garlic bulb

- Ginger root
- Licorice
- Mullein root
- Oregon grape stem bark or root bark

- Stinging nettle leaf
- Thyme
- Willow bark

Most of the PEP sand badge works in an apartment, except for the outside bits... So we adjusted the list and added a few more BBs to compensate.

In other words, by completing this badge, you are about 80% of the way to completing the PEP Sand badge and have a bit of a dent in the PEP Straw badge too!

Complete the following PEP BBs:

- ☐ Do laundry by hand
- ☐ Wash dishes without a dishwasher
- ☐ Clean a bathroom
- ☐ Clean a kitchen
- ☐ Clean an oily dish without soap
- ☐ Grease hinges
- ☐ Oil wooden kitchen utensils
- ☐ Get whiter whites without chlorine bleach
- ☐ Sweep a floor
- ☐ Make rags from old clothes
- ☐ Deep clean the fabric on a couch or chair using natural cleaners
- ☐ Manually clean an oven
- ☐ Set up a rag system
- ☐ Set up a cloth napkin system
- ☐ Make a general purpose natural cleaner
- ☐ Deep clean the interior of a refrigerator
- ☐ Deep clean the exterior of a refrigerator

Chapter 50
PEA Oddball

This aspect focuses on covering projects that don't quite fit elsewhere. Points are calculated the same as in the PEP Oddball badge with a PEX factor, Pro factor and Otis factor. The only difference is the number of points required.

The Sand badge is granted for a score of 7 points.

Chapter 51

Sand Badge in 5 Hours

In the spring of 2019, I hosted a two week informal PEP1 event (note: not a class, just a wild scramble to figure out a lot of the PEP stuff). Nobody ended up PEP1 certified. In fact, only a handful of people completed any badges. Lots of people took all the proper pictures and thought they would sort out badges when they got home.

On the last day we talked about what would be a reasonable expectation for how long it would take to get PEP1 certified at this pace. Since most people had completed about half of the BBs, they were thinking that it would be four weeks. They also felt strongly that we should eliminate all mention that a sand badge is an estimated 5 hours of experience – as that leads to some strong frustrations.

If there were a formal PEP1 course, fully staffed, with 12 students, then I think that a sand badge would generally fit into 5 hours for 3 of the students. Rather than lots of people having conversations about BBs, and people looking stuff up on YouTube or how-to sites, there would be an instructor telling you what, exactly, you need to know. And the tools would be laid out in front of you, and the instructor would provide guidance along the way.

An excellent example of all this is the club mallet (roundwood woodworking). One guy reported that it took him the better part of a day to make it. Another guy reported that it took him half an hour. Caleb Larson once told me that when you are making shakes with a froe, you burn through mallets so fast, you get used to making a lot of them. He said he can make a mallet in about seven minutes.

A Cord of Firewood

The price for a cord of firewood around here is about $200, delivered. Problematic wood is $170 and excellent wood might be $230. Two guys will drive out in the woods with a trailer and come back with 3 cords. This will take about six hours. They will then spend about 4 hours getting it delivered. Ten hours. They will take damn good care of their truck, saws, tools and everything because they need to end up with money in their pockets. 3 cords is $600. So each guy has a gross of about $300. If you figure in some tool burn, various fuels, wear and tear on everything… they did pretty good. Maybe better than $20 per hour.

A couple of years ago I hosted a rocket mass heater event and we didn't have nearly enough firewood. Three boots (in our permaculture bootcamp) went a hundred yards up the hill to harvest a dead standing tree. After two full days they managed to have a third of a cord stacked. A third of $200 is $67. Three people at eight hours per day for two days is 48 hours. That works out to about $1.39 per hour.

Last fall I paid a guy $250 for a cord of wood, cut and stacked. It was the first time he had ever harvested any firewood. His pickup, his saws, my trees. He did a good job. Exactly one cord stacked so nicely I hated to burn it. In the end, he said that he figures he earned about $10 per hour – but he learned a lot along the way. He thinks that for a second cord, he could get that to $15 per hour. Maybe.

PEP Is About Experience

Each sand badge is about five hours of experience. Maybe it will take a full week to get that five hours. Maybe a pro can crank it out in two hours. Some people learn faster than others. Rather than hide the "5 hours" I've decided to leave it and emphasize that it is about five hours of hands-on experience for a talented newbie. If there are 12 people at an event, the second fastest person will likely clock in at 5 hours.

We tried to hit "about five" for all badges. In the years to come, we might learn that some are closer to "three" or "nine." The good news is that no matter what the actual number is, everybody gets to suffer equally to earn the same badge.

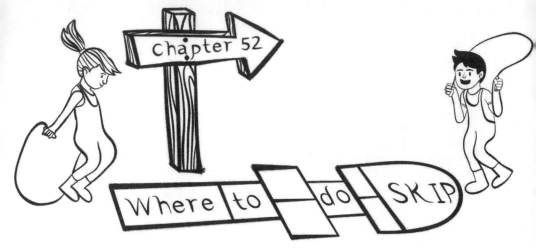

chapter 52

Where to do SKIP

A few people can do all of the BBs on their own homestead. Most people don't have access to a homestead, or their homestead might be missing some ingredients. What then?

The most obvious solution is that you could have a friend or relative who has the missing ingredients, or a church acquaintance or coworker. Put the word out that you want to cut firewood or dig a pond and someone is likely to take you up on it.

There are some people who will host a two or three day SKIP event and invite anybody over. As a result, they might end up with some firewood cut and stacked, and maybe an extra 3-log bench. Maybe a couple of nice gardening chores are taken care of. We are already hearing from some people planning to do this. I did something like this once and ended up with a lot of dry stack, about six three-log benches, a couple of kindling crackers and loads of chores knocked out.

I once hosted a BB20 event which was open to anybody with at least 20 BBs completed. This brought in people with a lot more skill. I ended up with even more high quality artifacts!

Most recently, I offered a two week course and it filled up quickly. It was a bit more formal. And by doing that we got a lot of ideas about an even more robust course.

Prospective Otises might want to offer their place for people to work on projects so they can vet candidates in person.

Check permies.com/t/97759 for a list of places where you can do PEP. Or, maybe start a new thread expressing your wish for a site closer to you.

Building an entire wofati by yourself is difficult and can really test your ability to work alone. At the same time, eight people building a wofati together goes quickly, is more enjoyable and tends to build community.

Suppose a person puts seven months into helping seven different people build their wofatis (a month per person). And then builds their own wofati and gets the help of seven people for a month. Is it fair to say that they have the same experience in natural building as the person who did it solo? And look at all their added community experience! Might it also be fair to say that the coordinator of the arrangement "built" a bunch of community? It feels a bit like an Amish barn raising!

I call this a "Labor Investment Collective" or LIC. Somebody sets up a LIC and gets several people to participate. In the end, everybody gets one BB artifact and a stronger community.

A LIC is set up for a given BB. Another LIC can be set up for the same BB, maybe with more projects and fewer hours per project. A LIC requires proof of experience in all parts of the project.

Example LICs:

A: You help six people, one month each, build a wofati. And later, six people spend a month helping you build a wofati

B: You help four people, one week each, build a berm shed. And later, four people spend a week helping you build a berm shed.

C: You help two people build a rocket mass heater for the full build. Later, two people help you build a rocket mass heater for the full build.

Using example A: At your first build you meet Jane. This is Jane's build. Jane has helped six other people build wofatis. There are two other people there, Bob and Beth. Bob has helped with two other wofati builds, and this is Beth's first wofati build – like you. A week later, Bob leaves because he arrived several weeks earlier than you – Bob has put in his full month. The next week Beth leaves, because she has then put in her full month. The day after that, Emily arrives. Emily has helped with four other wofati builds and she will continue to help after you have left.

On your second wofati build, you arrive to find 12 people already there. And three more people arrive just as you arrive. For your entire month, many people come and go. Among those arriving, you see Beth again.

Your third build is hosted by Steve. It's just you and Steve for the whole month. Apparently one other person came a couple of months ago. And it looks like Steve might be finishing the build soon. So Steve helped with six other builds and it looks like Steve might not get as much help out as he put in.

You put three more months into three more builds. A month on each build. And then you start your build. You end up with 11 people helping you for a month each – spread out over two and a half months. You end up finishing the project earlier than you expected. You submit your BB showing pictures of all seven builds that you were a part of.

The person creating the LIC might get their project done first. They won't get their BB certified until they've helped enough people in the LIC. Whoever gets their artifact last will probably have the highest quality artifact because it was built with so much experience.

The general theory is that you put ten days in and get ten days back. If there is a lot of interest in the LIC, then you might get 20 days back. And if interest in the LIC has faded, you might get zero days back – in which case, all you got was an education on how to do this BB.

If you set up a LIC, there's a BB for that in the Community aspect...

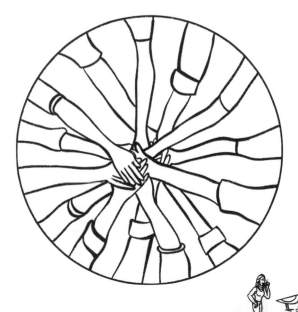

Featured Straw Badge BB:
Develop a LIC (Labor Investment Collective)

You will pull together a group of people and agree to a labor sharing arrangement. Examples could include:
- Each person contributes one month to helping others build a berm shed and gets back one month of others helping to build a berm shed.
- You and 4 people spend a day on each person's RMH build. When it's your turn, you promote the activity enough that a few extra people join in for the learning and fun. Thus, the LIC could continue after your contribution is over.

Clarification for BBs completed through a LIC
- Show that you did all the parts of a project over the course of your involvement
  - You can't just be the "cob monkey" for all the builds while someone else specializes in another part of the project

Minimum requirements:
- Create a LIC
- At least 3 BBs are completed and certified
  - Same BB
  - One of the BBs is yours
- At least 6 people invest labor with an expectation of repayment over the course of the LIC
- Each LIC must have a total time commitment (per person) of at least 40 hours and at least 8 hours per project

To document this Badge Bit, provide the following:
- Create a Permies.com thread documenting the creation and implementation of the LIC (must provide proof of meeting the above requirements)
  - Photo or video proof of participation in all the builds and you doing all the different parts of the builds

How much does SKIP cost?
By design, getting PEP certified is free.

Can I get to PEP4 if I'm vegan?
Yes! There are many paths to PEP4 that will work for vegans.

Do I need previous experience?
Nope! While it helps, the point of PEP is to build experience. You can build from zero.

Do I need tools?
Not to get started. If you need more tools than you currently have access to, chances are that you can be PEP1 certified without spending more than $100.

Do I have to have a farming background?
Nope. It's probably easier if you don't (less to unlearn).

Will I be famous?
Possibly. If you get to a higher level (PEP 2 and up) you'll have a following on Permies.com. If you're given Otis's land and you make that known publicly, you might garner some attention.

Is this like Scouts?
Yes, in a way. Scouts teaches you a lot of skills and being an Eagle Scout opens up doors. PEP teaches you a lot of different skills and being PEP2 or PEP3 might give you a door to live behind.

Are there other people doing SKIP?
You bet. At the time of writing this, 3740 BBs have been certified, 203 people have completed a badge and 2 people are PEP1 certified.

Are there any Otises?
Yes. Paul has met many, and heard from a couple dozen, some of whom passed away before they could find a suitable heir. Mike has heard from a dozen. Several have recently identified themselves to the program and their privacy is being guarded. At the time of this writing, we firmly believe that the first person to get PEP2 certified will have their pick of at least 20 different offers.

We think that there are millions of people like Otis. Every day more people are starting PEP and more Otises are finding out about PEP.

If the Otises are real, why don't you share a list of those you know about so we can verify it?
We started to do that, but the Otises got bombarded with "Will your land to me!" requests. Now the Otises stay quiet, but they're willing to open a line of communication with those they deem worthy.

Has anyone inherited property already?
We aren't aware of any yet.

What if I don't live in the US?
You can pursue PEP anywhere in the world. Currently over half the Otises we know about live outside the US.

What do I tell my parents?
"Let's see who gets to retire first!"

This is a new program that helps connect ambitious hard-working young people with older homesteaders so that they can inherit their homestead or farm. It can be done in parallel with normal working jobs with the chance of being able to avoid debt and live happily for the rest of your life. And your parents can come visit whenever they want.

Will this make me more employable?
Maybe? Proving that you can learn, follow directions and display your new skills could be attractive to an employer in some fields. If you fall in love with a particular aspect of PEP, say roundwood woodworking, you may dive into an employable field that you never would have known about.

Is this cheaper than getting a university degree?
Yes. Unless your university is free.

Can I do this with friends?
You bet! There are already avenues to connect with other PEP candidates within the Permies.com platform. You could form a PEP club or just do it with a couple friends. Just know that you need to do your own work for the BBs.

Can I do this part time?
Yes, it's particularly well suited to part time or seasonal availability.

Do I have to move?
Not to do PEP. If Otis gives you land you might want to move onto it.

Do I have to take Otis's land if he lives in the middle of nowhere?
No. How Otis bequeaths his land to you is up to him. It's likely he'd have a requirement that you live on the land for 5 years. But you could always turn down the offer.

Is PEP safe?
PEP/PEX is for tracking what you have done. It is not for teaching you how to do it, or how to do it safely. You will need a different book (or other resource) for that.

What electronic gear do I need to start SKIP?
You need to be able to take pictures/video and post them to Permies.com. Everything else is dependent upon which badges you want to pursue.

How do I get my SKIP activities verified?

Post the required pictures or videos to the appropriate BB thread on Permies.com to get that particular BB certified. Once you have all the BBs completed for a badge, post in the badge thread with links to all of your completed BB posts. Then someone can quickly verify whether or not you qualify for the badge. Hint: The ebook is filled with links to each appropriate BB thread.

Wheaton Labs

Do I need to do PEP at Wheaton Labs?

No. PEP is set up with the idea of it being able to do it remotely. Of course, there are a lot of cool things at Wheaton Labs that might be handy in getting some of the BBs done.

What if I can't do a BB where I am?

Developing a program that works for every person in every location would take decades. This program has been set up with the idea that it works perfectly at Wheaton Labs in Montana, with the idea that it will probably work really well for thousands of other properties. The goal is to make the program work at this level and then, eventually, maybe, consider expanding it out to more situations. So for now, if you can't do a BB where you are, you will need to go to a place where you can do it.

Where can I take a class?

We are working on increasing the frequency of PEP events at Wheaton Labs. And we hope that other people will start offering PEP events too.

Do I have to take a class?

No. The whole system is set up with the idea that it can be done at home with no formal instruction. Although, some people might enjoy a bit of extra instruction.... or an excavator.

How can I become qualified to teach a PEP class?

There is no official certification process for PEP teachers. Potential PEP students would likely appreciate seeing that the person who is teaching them has done those things before. So getting PEP certified yourself could be good preparation for teaching PEP. The key is that the BBs will still be posted and verified publicly on the Permies.com forums. The submissions for BBs will be reviewed on the forums and not necessarily by the individual teaching the class.

I have ideas for more BBs or changes. What should I do?

This program is evolving and will probably continue to be refined and improved for the next decade. We struggled with the decision of taking a "snapshot" of it right now, even though it's not perfect, versus waiting years until it's fully refined. We chose to get it out into the world now.

Suggest your changes at Permies.com in the PEP Refinement Ideas thread.

I've been cooking for 25 years. Why can't you just give me an Iron Badge in Food Prep and Preservation?

Have you read the requirements for the Iron badge in Food Prep and Preservation? If we gave you the badge it would defeat the purpose of demonstrating your skills to Otis.

Because of your experience, the entire process will be far easier for you.

A BB on Permies.com looks different from what's in this book – what's up with that? Can I still get credit if I did what the book said?
No. The book is a snapshot in time. The BBs, badges, and requirements may change over time, so Permies.com is the best place to verify you're doing tasks correctly.

This book is an attempt to introduce you to the concepts of SKIP and PEP – but the real meat is at Permies.com.

A BB or a badge on Permies.com changed since I was approved for it. Does my work still count?
Yes. If the requirements change after your work was approved, your BB or badge still counts.

The requirements for XXX seem really hard, complicated or require expensive equipment. Why are you making this so hard?
A challenging BB means it has higher value once it's completed.

What's a BBV?
BBV stands for Badge Bit Verification. They act as cumulative points and allow SKIP to support itself. You earn a BBV when you approve a BB for someone else. You may lose a BBV if your BB gets rejected. You may need a certain number of BBVs to become PEP1 certified.

When can I approve other people's BBs and badges?
You can approve others when you have earned that BB yourself and you have earned the Sand badge for that aspect.

I made a meal for 8 people but had a bit of help from my sister. That's still ok, right?
No.

Can someone else take the pictures for me and post on my behalf?
No.

Can I get approved for a task I did 20 years ago?
Yes, if you can provide the documentation that matches the BB requirements.

Does a 12 foot hugelkultur (Straw) also give me credit for the 6 foot hugelkultur (Sand)?
Nope. Unless specifically stated, doing one BB does not partially count towards another BB within that aspect.

- Examples:
  - Harvesting apples for the Sand badge of Foraging doesn't count towards the "Forage 100,000 calories" in the Wood badge of Foraging.
  - Baking a pizza for the Food Prep Sand badge could also earn you the "Cook with a Rocket Oven" in Rocket Sand and "Prepare a meal for 8" in the Community Sand badges.
  - The Gardening Wood badge requires growing 1 million calories of food, and the Iron badge requires 4 million calories. The food grown for the Iron badge is all new food – so you will have grown 5 million calories total.

Can I have help with my BBs?

Yes and no. If you need brute strength or a second set of hands to help you achieve a task, that's fine. You can't have someone else doing portions of the task that are building experience/skills for them instead of you. If the BB is to dig a pond, you need to dig the pond. If the BB is to put a log on a hugelkultur scaffolding you can have a hand getting it up there.

Check out chapter 53 for information about LIC where there is a way to participate in some group efforts.

Are there ways to track my progress?

Yes, check out:
- Ash Jackson's PEP Badge Tracker
- R Parian's BB Calculator for Google Sheets
- Merit badge profile on a user's profile at Permies.com

What's an "edge case" classification mean on my BB?

It means it's not clearly certifiable. It's not approved or rejected. You can add pictures or polish up your artifact and improve your submission to get it approved.

Could I create a PEW (for Walter) on Permies.com and have some overlap with PEP?

Yes. Eventually we expect there to be PEXs for many different permaculture philosophies and parts of the world.

Why aren't banana circles in the Gardening badge?

The current gardening badge is part of PEP which is cold climate focused. Bananas don't grow in a cold climate.

In time, a new PEX will probably be defined which includes banana circles.

Why didn't you make PEP more universal?

We talked about this a lot. What you see in this book turned out to be about 40 times more difficult than what we thought it would be. And making something that would work universally would probably be about 60 times more difficult than this, plus it would be really bulky and challenging to understand.

We hope that in ten years there will be dozens of PEXes that will make SKIP a better fit for folks who wish for PEP to be more universal.

How does the PEP system support itself if it's free?

Volunteers have created the system and are certifying BBs. People who have earned badges can approve other BBs. Earning higher level certifications will require participants to certify others for their BBs.

The foundation of PEP and SKIP is a massive gift from all of the volunteers and donors who made it happen.

I think I'm an Otis. How do I pick an heir?

There are many ways. Here are a couple:
- Review PEP candidates, find one you like and start a conversation.
- Post a land share or work trade opportunity on Permies.com requiring a certain PEP level to apply. Hopefully it will lead to a happy relationship.

Can I be an OTIS without a cool homestead?
Yes! Bequeathing money to a PEP candidate to allow them to buy a homestead in the area of their choice is a wonderful way to help aspiring homesteaders get onto the land.

Bequeathing money to PEP candidates who already have a place will also help them to stay on the land and not have to work a day job to keep living the permaculture dream.

How do I evaluate or vet the PEPpers?
That's currently up to you. The easiest ways are to:
- Look through the badges for things you care about (Metalworking, Textiles, etc.) and look for people who have received those badges.
- Click on the PEPper's name and go to their Merit Badge Profile to see what BBs/Badges they've done.
- Put a "watch" on a PEPper so you can get notified of their posts. Then you can see their BB submissions and their other posts so you can get to know them vicariously.

Where do I get legal documents to transfer my land to a PEPper? Also, I want them to start living here now – what paperwork do I need?
We have thoughts in this space, but for every case there are dozens (hundreds?) of variables for the Otis and the PEPper. Then comes a buffet of different laws in different countries and different states – maybe even counties and cities. You both need to choose how much documentation you want, and whether you want lawyers to look over your paperwork. As a free service, we just don't have the resources to give much, if any, advice.

How do I know if a PEPper is good or bad?
Reading their posts is a great way to get a feel for a PEPper. Having them come to your place for a visit may be another good way to vet someone. Background checks or other methods could also be worth investigating if you're getting serious.

How do I know a PEPper isn't trying to fleece me?
Not sure. A PEP3 candidate will have put in an awful lot of time and effort to get to that point. Without knowing their potential Otis, it would be a rather long con.

Chapter 55 — Acknowledgments

The idea for all of this popped into my head in October of 2014. I couldn't stop thinking about it. In January of 2015 I worked with **Jesse Markowitz** to create the earliest version of PEP badges and BBs. Later I subjected **Jocelyn Campbell** and **Fred Tyler** to hours and hours of my ramblings and calculations including a full overhaul of the system. In October 2017 I announced the new format and started getting feedback. This new framework became the foundation for what we have now.

While working on a Kickstarter with **Shawn Klassen-Koop** in 2018, we decided we needed a smaller ebook to be offered at the $1 reward level. We decided the small ebook would be about PEP. So we made a pass at defining all of the sand badges. This effort turned out to be about 20 times bigger than we anticipated. But I think the results were rather excellent. In May 2019 we touched page 1 of Kickstarter's most funded nonfiction books page.

Several people volunteered to create BBs and help with brainstorming content for the badges. The growth was organic, and it quickly felt like a mob was carrying me to get all this stuff done. Many of the BBs took several hours to properly define. And then about a quarter of the BBs ended up on the cutting room floor. Most of the sand badges Shawn and I created were overhauled to better fit the new framework.

In the Spring of 2019, about a dozen people came and spent two weeks at my place doing BBs. **Mike Haasl** played a bit of a leadership role – and a lot of the PEP program morphed during this event to better follow reality. In the Fall, we tried something similar. **Ash Jackson** and **Ashley Lortscher** participated. Through a lot of 2020, the four of us met regularly to further define PEP and SKIP.

Mike Haasl became a large driving force for the whole project, including the Kickstarter! So much so that you can see his name on the cover!

David and Andrés Bernal contacted us shortly before the Kickstarter. They made the Kickstarter video, did the illustrations, book cover, sexy centerfold, layout and a long list of fun things for this book. They're part of **The Bernal Brothers Studio** along with Daniela, Sonia, and Nestor.

A group of passionate textiles enthusiasts spent hundreds of hours refining the Textiles aspect and creating BBs with carefully crafted requirements, sizes and material types. Their product is what we hope the rest of the badges could look like someday.

Dozens of people helped write BB poetry and fill out the badge content on Permies.com. Each BB took 5 to 30 minutes to craft. There are around 1350 BBs in PEP.

People who helped with the early ebook:
- Shawn Klassen-Koop
- Raven Ranson

People who reviewed the book and provided feedback:
- Ashley Lortscher
- Opalyn Rose
- Paul Fookes
- Sam Bang
- Raven Ranson
- Sharon Etchieson
- Katie Lefevre
- Maureen Abram
- Mary Clayton
- Leigh Tate
- Trevor Blankenship
- Katie Young
- Malek Ascha
- Kevin Roberts
- Jane Lewis
- Cara Hettich
- Ash Jackson
- Alan Booker
- Grey Klein

People who helped define the badges:
- Julia Winter
- Raven Ranson
- Andrea Klassen-Koop
- Jocelyn Campbell
- Fred Tyler
- Ashley Lortscher
- Ash Jackson
- Jennifer Richardson
- Opalyn Rose
- Nicole Alderman
- Chris "Uncle Mud" McClellan
- Kirk "Donkey" Mobert
- Jay Angler
- Judith Browning
- Vera Vil
- Carla Burke
- Robin Katz
- Tracy Wandling

People giving us handy advice:
- Alyssa Cleland
- Leigh Tate
- Kate Downham

Nicole Alderman designed the cool badge images!

Pioneers in helping the program get moving:
- Opalyn Rose
- Nicole Alderman
- Ashley Lortscher
- Beau Davidson
- Leigh Tate
- Fred Tyler
- Penny McLoughlin
- Inge Leonora-den Ouden
- Rob Lineberger
- Kevin Harbin
- David Huang
- Julie Harris
- Jordan Barton
- Zoe Ward
- Cam Lee
- Rebecca Blake
- R Parian
- Mike Barkley
- Kate Downham
- D. X. Logan
- Steve Thorn
- Ash Jackson
- Dawn West
- Andrea Locke
- Dave Burton
- Raven Ranson

People who helped create BB pages:
- Dave Burton
- Steve Thorn
- Daron Williams
- Ash Jackson
- Liv Smith
- Nicole Alderman
- Raven Ranson
- Kirk "Donkey" Mobert
- Leigh Tate
- Opalyn Rose
- Lesley Verbrugge
- D. Logan
- Kevin Harbin
- Inge Leonora-den Ouden

Chapter 56

This Is a Crowdfunded Book

We made a free thing and people asked for it to be mashed into a book. Our response was "Nobody is gonna pay for a book made of stuff you can have for free." They said "We will pay!" and "Gimmie, gimmie, gimmie!" To prove our point, we set up a Kickstarter and said "If you really want a book, then put up the coin! This stuff costs money ya know?" And they put up the coin. 2,575 people put up $148,817. About 15 times more than most books get over their entire lifetime. I guess people really do want a book about something that is available for free. I hope that we added enough extra content to the book to make it worth the money.

There are moments when the world seems to be an unending river of unkindness. It makes the idea of fleshing out this wacky idea feel like utter folly. But suddenly more than a hundred people jump in to help with all the work. And a couple thousand more shove dollars into your pocket and give you a pat on the back.

It's a beautiful world we live in
A sweet romantic place
Beautiful people everywhere
The way they show they care

-- Devo

I'm so happy. I'm so grateful. I hope to make lots more fun projects. Thanks to all the wonderful people who threw coin into this Kickstarter.

Thanks to our Magnificent Kickstarter Supporters

MashGrapeDarlingEssBeeNer
Michelle and Dakota Burris
Rex "Reximus Prime" Reeves
Christopher Andrew Holloway
Kneebiter Coydon Wallingham
Matthew "Antonovka" Johnson
Hugo & Victor Future Heroes
Nancy Perez And Kathy Riser
Brother from another Mother
Lori Rizzo, Aristaios Farms
Ash Jackson & Arthur Jackson
Mac the Wookie AKA PaPai-Wan
PELİN TASER CHİCAGO İSTANBUL
Jan G. Chief Technical Wizard
Eric "The Mad Farmer" Tolbert
Kathy Bacon and Clinton Jones
Minjsasassin soap making ninja
Literati Press Comics & Novels
Bradlington Von Blocksdorfford
Greg Brown del Rancho los Gatos
Christopher "BUDDHAMONKe" Hadley
Finch Frolic Garden Permaculture
Gaia Gate Landing & Carole Sumler
Josh Ricks, Jackass Extraordinaire
Hugginn, Munninn and Odin Thank You.
AnnaLea Kodiak of the Shattered Anvil
Grey Gardner and the crew of Serenity
Tyler & Andrea & George & Arthur Young
The Gray Ghost Goatherder and his herd
Fergie @ South Mountain Permaculture Lab
Denise Spencer, caretaker of Shiloh Pines
Ho-Sheng Hsiao and the Hsiao Family
Mamá Merce Morris - Panamá - Por mis hijos
Northeast Ohio Skillshare Reedsandroots.org
Mike Detienne, Owner Micron Enterprises LLC
The Tame Dwarf from Sand Hollow Homestead :)
Chieftess Dirty-Neck and her Neverwash Tribe
Watered Ridge Farmstead, Edwardsburg, Michigan
Hogeye Farm's Harry & Merry from Hogeye, Texas
Lisa Orr and her Pottery Permaculture Paradise
Ryan Halik, asker of questions, doer of things.
Jennifer Pomykaj- Head Farmer at Triple P Farms
The Un-Bamboozle Adventure Game www.TUBAgame.com
Gringo Bellaco de Santa Fe (Col. Braya Panawaty)
Raymond and Rachael Faber with Sarigrace and Hope
Katie, Carl, and Lily Young: Blue Feather Homestead
kokosbonny who is not angry anymore because of permies
Mariah Mother of Coyotes and Moons Moncada, also Colten

RobK
Moli
Pops
Anikó
mknife
Donald
Richard
Tsuga!!
patrick
Kyle Noe
KarenJoy
Mitchmon
Uncle Mud
Akkaydrah
RJ Vinson
DJ Bowers
Just Brad
anonymous
Chris Sugg
Davin Hoyt
Jay Skiles
E.T. Mings
Pat DeLang
Logan Byrd
Diane Cohn
Terranitup
Red Dragon
Mercurious
Oakie James
Artie Scott
Justin Otis
JDWheeler42
Dave Burton
Michael Tullius

luke iseman
Adam Barehl
Malek Ascha
Tracy Popey
DocinChrist
Cable Jones
tblankinship
MATTY BOI!!!
Randy Martin
Teresa Meyer
Abhi Agarwal
Joe Gesualdi
Grandma Gail
Otto Trebing
Daniel Bryan
E-Ricky Ticky
Bram Wijgerde
Kevin Roberts
3 Bar W Farms
All 6 Schicks
Bobboe T.E.M.
Craig Taffaro
Bryce Johnson
Julie Francis
Thadius Marcus
frankdugan.com
Kenneth Elwell
Ann Socolofsky
Catskill Frank
Brian Ferguson
Esther Allerton
Louis G. Weiner
Project Anavita

Lorrie L Henson
Mark D Anderson
prphasmnr kydio
Obsidian Novica
Brittany Hoover
mastodonfood.com
Jackrabbit Megee
Ellison Farms WV
Dylan Countryman
Find compassion.
Aric Donajkowski
Jonathan Lawrence
The Shimel Family
Mike The Majestic
Justin Litchfield
Golden Acorn Farm
Sarah of the Doans
The Feral Mx Maddy

Rebecca Dahl Cookston
Nick "MacGyve" Tedford
John & Michelle Valdes
church of Christ Farms
Ryan Frederick Gilmore
Tom@blackhillswild.com
BubbaSchottMiles Farms
Ocelot & Rook McPherren
Angela Lynn Montes: Yap
Nathaniel Bryce Blevins
The Inimitable CS Lukacs
The Rhodes (Eco)Warriors
The Mackay Clan in Japan
Marta of Wolfenwald Farm
chanel says blessthisish
Stacie and Michael Weber
charles "goat man" smith
Copperhead Road Homestead
Alejandro Prieto Carrizal

Plant Person Pivik
Tutor the Barbarian
Wayne F-ing Shannon
Jausawaeth Borsteth
Richard Kicklighter
Aron & Amy Eldridge
onespiritualpitcher
H. Michael Rauscher
Golden Valley Acres
Stephen Bruno Thomas
Rachel Borawski-Rudd
Rebelbeefcompany.com
Vernon L. Sanders II
Hungry Hawk Homestead
Lovey Rita Meter Maid
That Knife Guy Daniel
brunettegardens.com
Dancing Garden Beeing

Dana "Can't think of anything clever to put here" Martin
David Huang doer of things at www.theartisthomestead.com
Alexandra Malecki, Master of Curiosity and Troublemaking
Brigitte Melchert, member of the Crazy Chicken Lady clan!
Janie Brackett: MOTHER, Domestic Goddess, Chicken Wrangler
Laura R, RN - looking for ways to improve community health
Jessica Eckman of Treehouse Farms from the humble town of Utahn!
Kenneth Kirkpatrick, Purveyor of Pasties, Pizza & Pies on a patio.
Kevin Calvey, Catholic homeschooling father of 7 & permaculture fan
Gulas Family - Derek and Briana, Eli, Jaiden, Stephen, and Benjamin
Rainmaker, soil grower, connector - her Earthal Fixership the Polymath.
Keith Pagett "Husband, father, preacher, man. Serving all as best I can!"
John, at FuelLoadManagement.com Forestry Mulching, Brush Goats, Fire Lines
Mother, kinder teacher, permaculturalist, massage therapist extraordinaire!
Chris, Liz, Emily, CJ, Annie, Sweet Caroline, Ellen, Josh, MawMaw and Kudo.
xDrFirefly & LJ | Hen-X { The Mavis Institute } Flat Top, WV #PorchBees4life
Chad/Tabitha Zimmerman and their 10 mostly wonderful Kids in Wisc. + Lila/Daisy
Richmond Park Farm - Polled A2 Dairy Heritage Shorthorns - North Idaho Landrace
Callan Maclin Siobhan Alec The whole world on a tiny hilltop with love forever.
EcoPig: Long Lost Pig #4 with SKIP world domination knowledge to outwit the BBW!
Vic, Servus Cordis Jesu Sacratissimi et Cordis Mariae Immaculati, Orate Rosarium

RD	Dave Deft	Ry Thompson	Zoe Ward (UK)	Drager Farms, LLC
No	Ken Corey	Billy Magee	Molly Shields	Chupmunk Snuggles
Bod	Josh Gray	The Mammoth	Gordon Walton	Sonja D. Williams
TAP	Adam Roth	The T House	fVern Fingiez	Daring Faith Farm
CAJ	Dusti Jay	Cory Shires	Vasara family	Annie Daellenbach
sid	Alex Pine	Dali Aquino	Henri & Cloée	Susan Elaine Kite
AGS	Ben Hylen	Blacksmokin	Alex Koloskov	BushelsNPecks.com
Yan	The Nutes	Obi the Chi	Karol Hartley	Dominic M Crolius
Pipo	Carole Ly	Team Awesome	Linda Randall	Kirsten Mouradian
Mimi	Addy Rain	Kevin Harbin	Rebekah Kirby	Manuel Ray Garcia
B.H.	The Hooks	Lord Tidwell	Mahabba Meyer	Thomas B. Jackson
Coco	Samiamias	Bryan Wetzel	Bill Erickson	Lady Carola Meyer
Marv	Mugen Bear	Barbara Tada	Spencer Bowen	Bryan de Valdivia
Zoran	Mare Silba	Honey Badger	Jess Mcdonald	John and Amy Dyer
Chupi	Sunny King	Kate Downham	ChuckandToots	Barbra and Alyssa
Chris	Derek Cate	Jeremy Irwin	Martin Hommel	Third Farm Bakery
Grant	Zenblaster	Steven Every	Anny the Grok	Andrew Willerding
Patch	Leigh Tate	Ron Jacobson	Heather Allen	BlessedbyBees.com
Linzi	R L DeMint	Ryan Haffele	Nan from Yaak	Benjamin R Conway
ppetru	KJS Olesen	Aaron Powell	Oliver Strano	Wm. David Randall
AZMIKE	Permiegirl	Andy Commons	Colonel Zimka	Jonathan E Kinsey
Jordan	Jonas Berg	jOsH aWeSoMe	Nancy McClain	Luke Dinklefarmer
J.Ruiz	Bryan Tran	Dragan Smith	Jason Learned	The Vibranium Chef
MrRobi	Tim Bermaw	Off-Grid Guy	Jake Robinson	Pasquale DeAngelis
Kyle B	Rod Hoover	Kasey Wooten	Isa Pavilonis	Robert and Lisa B.
G.R.C.	Ryan Burns	Becky Fisher	Tolin Simpson	Bess @ Willowsedge
Brento	Joey Means			Andrew Roy Jackman
T Rowe	Jeff Dible			Pfaffke van Oilsjt
hyfall	Candy Loam			Enjoy-The-Farm.com
Alan M	Kim Arnold			Shane DeMeulenaere
Lowtek	Sarah B xx			www.missionmet.com
Rooter	Farmer Sam			Lois Blood Bennett
MarMil	Terry Wren			James M. A. Schick
Kapena	Jeff Swart			Matthew A Bredeson

Elkin W	Myers Gray	Damian Degus	Evan Epperson	I do not want this
GordieM	Eric Kucks	Matt Tomasov	Jonnigallante	Soil Solutions LLC
C. Edie	The Wookie	Dr. Ken Crum	Jesse C Styer	Iconic Ironic Ilse
G Cronk	Nihal Özen	Rudy Valvano	Esellie Laing	Scott E. Nicholson
Druid57	Tim Rooney	Pippa Knight	Chris Hoffert	ReditusNatural.com
CARLOSG	All4Rasmus	Jin Sung Kim	Familia Hoche	Fredrik Chronqvist
TJ King	The Merles	Adams_way_IG	Ashia Lyralin	Romeo J. Doganetti
C. Dant	ElCocoLoco	Paul Pittman	James Bassett	Eric Addison Bakey
Danimal	Rabbi Adam	Shawn Werber	Azra Bertrand	Your Friend Mariah
F. Skip	Fil Garpet	PizzaGod9000	Brian Seibert	Justin Elkan Jones
Mardell	Brian Tant	Herbalicious	James K. Mick	Missus Robyn Graves
BonnieM	PocketTurd	Chez LaBelle	Avalon Family	Goran the gravehawk
Kiirkas	Ella & Seb	Joshua Arney	Banished_Rural	Jared Neal McCurrin
Amira A	Tilia Milo	ol man Quack	Peter of SZOSZ	Healthy Earth Farms
Penny Mc	Jurriaan S.	Eric Merrill	Amanda Prévost	Dori, like the fish
MesaLisa	nova wright	Iviana Bynum	Dan Broockmann	Jakub Préma Podlaha
Chervock	Granny Crow	Tom Behrmann	Herring Family	Larseroo the Firste
Samariah	Thea Flurry	Nick Dawbarn	the Van Meters	A. Cupp of Sunshine
Vasilyev	Anita Bueno	Erin Vaganos	Sandy Sabatino	Central Scrutinizer
Byt3G04t	Hadesmonger	Jason Tuller	Kirsten McEvoy	Derek and Tara Holt
Lori Ott	Lew Johnson	Dolly Sparks	Peter Luitjens	Spartacus the Dragon
mahBarker	Sean Wilkie	Colin Endean	Daniel Tiecher	VeganJoe Bourguignon
Bret Mayo	Andrew Butt	Scott Hudson	Aaron Jamieson	Tim the Newgardenguy
BethHoney	Barry Neish	Mike Reinard	Davey Campbell	Candace of Willhaven
For Pyrat	Mammabearog	Scott Conroy	Nomis Reremmak	Scarlet & the Olives
Icon Lady	Tim DiCarlo	Cam & Minnie	Famille Landry	Silke Van der Stockt
Rory Moon	Robert Pane	Jen Cochrane	Henk van Doorn	The Devletian Family
Brandon R	Grumbleweed	Colin Rogers	Barefoot Jenna	Jim Smij.com Siefert
Pluttjack	Chris Allen	Rikard Gehlin	Nataly Marchuk	Ravens Way Homestead
Arjen Bos	Brandon Lee	Dixie M Davis	Momma Talmarie	DrewMatchuosaurusRex
Doug Dodd	Richie Ring	Renegade D.I.	Lazy Owl Acres	Forest Haven Academy
Mama Bear	Jose Castro	Amy and Ember	Derek Frerichs	Victoria Lambakakhar

177

Álvaro Herrera
AndroitFrisson
Zalman Kuperman
Michael Freeman
Arliss Wirtanen
NateMisbehavin'
Justin Gonzales
Claudia Shimkus
Dewayne Cushman
Dana O'Driscoll
Silvanus Rempel
Sergio Crovetto
Tracy J. Steele
Eileen D. Armes
Gredlic Bronder
Empress Arachne
Justin Credible
Andrej Anderlič
Martin le malin
Awen Skywatcher
Alex from malta
Gramma Pancakes
Brent M. Hardin
Michael LaRusch
Peace Creek Peg
Michael Leonido
James C. Wilson
Michael Pongrac
Mrs. Incredible
C.D. Stephenson
Robert Schwartz
Tyler W. Howard
Brent Chriswell
MLM Sawing Wood
J.R. Hinostroza
Old Man Brennan
Sergi Caballero
David Treebeard
Jānis Štālbergs
Douglass family
The Woodbutcher
Cynthia Silveri
Justin Nafziger
Kaloko Gardener
Becky Weisgerber
Rojer with a "J"
Jocelyn Campbell
Sir Earl of Beer
Crafty Lady Lyda
www.campchet.com
The Crimson Chin
Albert D Johnson
Shelley R. Stark
Martin Steinberg
Humee Hum Huynhs
Tobi-Wan Kernobi
Burnt Sky Family
Yoost the Aussie
Sharon Elkington
Valerie + Ramsey
John Evan Farmer
Valerie K. Vines
Seth Wolschlager
Paul C Ellsworth
Joylynn Hardesty
Cangrejo Arbóreo

Terra Silva Curantis
Rocketstovecores.com
William J Conroy, III
Andy from Kansas City
Hollowbrook Homestead
The Pinenuts in Idaho
Rob@anthillliving.com
Anton & Maja Puščavar
Beely Hua Hua Shmoooo
Proverbs 1:7, 8:11-12
Emperor Aimee Cabrera
LaughingDuckRanch.com
Dillon & Ashley Novak
Kate And Evan Mitchell
Jodahs Caoimhe Shepard
Audrey Butterfly Smith
Professor John C. Fish
Mark, Jo, Eva and Elie
Tyron & Jamie Baltazar
The Horde of Ballhalla
Trees of Darkness Farm
Kirk & Chelsea Johnson
Mr. Bubba and Lunakins
Teaglach O'Cuinneagain
Glenn and Gina Haggard
Greg The Mineral Fixer
Edgar Julian Caballero
AKU.si Klemen Urbanija
Salish Sea Islandrover
Ralph the Wonder Llama
Hunter & Jacinda Stark
Woodland Craft Supplies
Bob & Stephanie Frenock
Mike and Megan Koeniger
Rich and Patti Quintano
Little Biggi Lighthouse
The Worthless Professor
Cascadia Forest Therapy
Jackie & Dan Knaulsgard
Nina & Thomas Viereckel
Indra Bishop, the Furry
Robert "Busky" Northrup
Tigercello Permaculture
Josh and Jenny Feathers
Kathryn Elizabeth Ossing
Ingeborg Kristina Palmer
RubyAnn & Michael Gaglio
Zach Hild (Hildaculture)
PLANE EARTH PERMACULTURE
Stelios Moschos "smosgr"
-= R F A =- PrimeTracker
www.MiGranitoDeArena.org
Barbara M Miller of NetM
Zachary March of Toronto
Priest of Purrrmaculture
Tea of The Northern Woods
Gloryland Ranch & Retreat
tomcat of Red Earth Farms
Roy Ramey of Avalon Farms
Freeman Sean Timothy Wood
YogaAyurvedaExplained.com
Pleasant Valley Community
Barry Chapman SW Oklahoma
The Plante's + Uncle Joel
Buddy Lindsey (BudDIY.net)
www.HandcraftedArtists.com

The artist formerly known as Duckpig
Mx. Bee of the Oakridge Tranarchists
Mx. Christopher J. and Lu R. Lo Coco
Cameron Kelvin Carter, la mente verde
Only Punxsutawney Phil's Shadow Knows
Kissing Cousins Farm, Grand Ledge, MI
Leah Esther, Land Hungry Plant Killer
Matthew Fien Gretton, Fungal Overlord
Vernon Inverness, the Triumphant One!
Captain Ohm Leader of the Resistance!
World's Handsomest Engineer - Kyle Bob
Sébastien Roy, PhD, wizard in training
Jubilee + Jasper + Radiance + Endeavour
Pawpaw GNOME Nursery @ McKenzie Gardens
David Benoit - Reconciliation Homestead
John -Jesus follower, husband and father
RENÉ & LESLEY VERBRUGGE NORMANDIE FRANCE
Josh & Adel Boschma, Bluehill Ridge farm
Shepardess at Old Schoolhouse Creek Farm
Matt and Hannah of St Spyridon Farmstead
Laura, Tinkerer in Chief @alchemyacres.ca
The Weird and Wonderful Nutty Nurse Averi
Jerry & Sage Webster, Innisfree Homestead
Jason alliwanttodoisplayinthesoil Guidone
Cate & Mark from Mawson Canadian Homestead
C. Justin Lawson of DewittPermaculture.com
Sir Michael Wayman, Rightful King of Saturn
Michael Roth - Kingdom Builder, Storyteller
Dan Patan, Shadow Governor of West Vertucky
undaunted6 The Magnificent Lord of Scotland!
Leif Ing, esposo de Lily, papi de Caleb y Ana
Linda and Jeff from Harmony Canyon New Mexico
Stephanie from Art of Special Needs Parenting
The honourable esteemed Alan Griffin aka AliG
Scot & Suzanne Cantrell Keepers of The Valley
Beau M. Davidson, Laird Family Farm, Harper KS
Robert And Lanell Jones form Melbourne,Florida

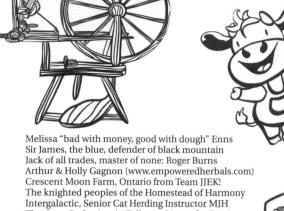

Paulie Dineen *jazz hands*
Shan Moon Goddess Lawrence
Jaizki Arteagabeitia Perea
Ahren "Daddy Bigz" Spilker
James and Katherine Veazey
Bumfuzzled Glynn-Ives gang
El Supremo CandyGram4Mongo
Rancho Gallina Eco-Retreat
Rick English, HoundFarm.com
The Nice Incredible Baxters
James Freeman & Robyn Perry
In Memory of Cynthia Siarny
Illegal Toaster of Tatooine
Cindi, Daughter of the Land
Lynne Marie Tognoni Keating
The Wonderful Widdows of Oz
Ambrosia Regen John Stupica
Left of Center Homesteading
Jodi- The Reverent Homestead
Elder Millennial Thaumaturgy
Chelsea from Lemon Tree Hill
The Viking from the Emmental
We are not men. We are Devo!
The Magnanimous Amanda Bello
Jerry Kranz, Christ-follower
Shaun "SurvivalStudent" Hill
Ryan "The Mycologeek" Dagley
Jason Bray, Eden Restoration
The Library Kailyn and Ahmed
Sir Matthew James Brown, Esq.
Heinrich Rentsch, Switzerland
Karri & Max – Chuckwagon Farm
Dusty from Little Window Farm
Cowgirl Carmen and Compatriots
Dave Bryant @ Somerset Landing
Sir Not Appearing In This Book
Alistair 'Hurricane' Hemingway
FarmerLarsson, Hope Creek Farm
Dr. Indy Ishaya, Spinal Wizard
Willow Creek Permaculture Farm
The Texas Sasquatch, Nathan T.
Andrew Schrenk, Renaissance Man
Andrea Locke (Nine Worlds Farm)
Kristine Keeney and Gary Walker
Phil Capobianco, Dominus Allium
Garth 'run the experiment' Wolf
Lord Adam & Lady Ashley Nilsson
Professor Alexander Smith, Ph.D.
Johnathan Michael Dulawan (JMAD)
Canadian Union of Frogs Local 52
Heather at High Desert Homestead
Barbara J. Roberts Healing Hands
Niveragain in the Final Frontier
VegAne af Knoltren Gaard, Norvegr
Barbara "Dixiemoon" Robiolio Bose
Big Bad Muthuh from Mullinalaghta
For my dad, Wendell Dwight Drennan
Simran-Prem-Singh-Peter-Schoendorf
Darlene Leeson Ninja Snake Shifter
Dave "I aim to misbehave" Thompson
The one and only, Za-y-va Lareche!
Moon River Ranch CSA - Clinton, MT
Lulu Lay, Goddess of the Summer Sky
Chris Paglinco & Heather Harrington
Griffin Radulski and Rosa the Brave
Josh "The Procrastinator Pro" Rimmer

Melissa "bad with money, good with dough" Enns
Sir James, the blue, defender of black mountain
Jack of all trades, master of none: Roger Burns
Arthur & Holly Gagnon (www.empoweredherbals.com)
Crescent Moon Farm, Ontario from Team JJEK!
The knighted peoples of the Homestead of Harmony
Intergalactic, Senior Cat Herding Instructor MJH
The Great Ryder Austin Zollman, Pirates for Ever!
neopolitan6, a fine musical chord, but very nerdy
Queen Pooella, Majestic Unicorn of Amethyst Manor
Pauper Pat the prodigal plum proliferator - Saint
Ashley Cottonwood - Reading Books & Raising Chooks
Dancing Pig Farms - witnesses and co-choreographers
Wishing you well. Best wishes to all. Jerry Beattie
Shaun Michael Daniel, Possessor of Three First Names
Join Hearts and Souls Together! lovepeaceharmony.org
Servant and son of the original permaculturalist. Tim
the Masterful Visionary Tony Grguric aka "toekneegee"
Lord of Stony Ridge Suburban Farms, Sir Jeff McIntyre
Paul Tipper and Deb Montague's farm without a name yet
Chuck & Amanda Reeves / Mountain View Farms of Cherokee
Sophie "Hi I'm Sophie" Lacson & Jonathan "Tamok" Engeln
The man that was once known as Chris "Six Slash" Schlack
Brent Paschall, Keeper of the Apiary of Infinite Buzzing
John Sechrest, Graand Poohbaah and builder of the future.
Wendy the Crazy Plant Lady O'Neill (Killing it in Zone 3!)
Bob "Jack of all Trades" and Gretchen "Lambie" Support Team
Brian & Kylie McFall and their wild tribe of 4 small people

179

Mighty Strengthor, His very name bulges with mighty strength
Corey always waiting until the last possible moment Sheppard
Vice Overlord of Vibration, James the Audio Visual technician
Brian Moyers - Ambassador to the Future at Back-to-Basics, LLC
The Fuzz - Breaker of Spines, Bringer of Hope, Agent of Change
Markku Salmela mid-boreal farm scale permaculture practitioner
^..^ -- A Permie from Central Valley - the Golden State :D ^..^
PASSERELLE ÉCO, www.passerelleco.info & www.ecovillageglobal.fr
Only The Best & Nothing Less www.GenesisPN.com Like God Intended
Tim, God father of the southern Illinois "Black Amish Mafia" hogs
Tim and Deborah from Nature's Gift Farms in beautiful North Idaho
Kamil, Alicja and Nella Gaia of the Southend in Transition commons
eLYE, idea wallah, 198555131*101*3, PS Ego vere non vis esse Deum.
Dolly, Jasper, Tilly, Elliot, Hodge, Keegan, Milo, Kirby and Lizzy
AresTactical.net Custom Holsters for Professionals and Adventurers.
Eric "the Red" Wagner the Offgrid ConSULTANt ioffgridding@gmail.com
Mrs Beezley (mother of the Mungalunga) and Sy (the bestest baby tapir)
Dave Madden and family, aspiring peasantry and lords of lazy composting
For Gretchen, Fredrick "Bubba", and Casey Bowles... Greatest Kids Ever!
J.Parker,The Dirtdad, Lord High Commander of the Realms of Mack Boulder
BBWB, Page 162, 2nd column, 9 lines up: She said yes. Wedding is 5/21/22.
wyldedges.com - Regenerative Education - Hertford, Hertfordshire, England
The Hartweg Family - Renaissance Earth: Farming • Alchemy • Ancestral Arts
Grant, Harrison, Elowen, and our Angel in Heaven are love and light eternal
Chad lewis-Cylinder Stoves.com portable camp stoves for heating and cooking
Blanche McBunch - Earthworm Surpriser, Catlap Provider and Fan o'Permies.com
Spencer, disturber of the kitten, the Pillar of Positivity, Bunziker-Helsvik
Erica Pope of the Wandering Bards & John Stephenson of Lost Adventurers Guild
Protect health & peace through healthy boundaries & self-sustaining practices.
Skot Colacicco, Pagan Minister. Heal the Land, Heal the Water, Heal the People
Memory of Mary & Norman Wiseman who lived through the depression and raised me
One Community Global - OneCommunityGlobal.org (epic sustainability superbacker)
Kevin Whitefield - www.idylllodges.co.uk building rammed earth lodges in the UK
Christina Wilson, Ohio Permie and Periodic Wanderer of Wild Roads Less Traveled
- Bennett R. S. Lynde, Husband and Father to the best family a man could ask for
A couple amazing sites with fun stuff to check out: THE3DER.COM & PUSHTOTECH.COM
Karyl Clark; descendant of many lovers of the land and all flora and fauna within
Donation in the name of Reddit commenter "Nohcri", who inspired me to take action
Grand Poobah, King of all that flies, swims and runs. The greatest Mike of all time
Jubilee Wylden Woolley-Fly ~ Gaia Goodness Growing Goddess Music Maker Cosmic Clown
Carla Burke, CoG, Happy-wifein', Critter-Snugglin', Gardenin', Herbalist, Extrordinaire

---

A note from one of our top backers

Gifts-Every seed-bearing plant & tree, every green plant for food. Water,
bread from earth, wine gladdens heart, oil makes faces glow, food sustains
strength. Let land rest every 7th yr. Harvest fruit tree 1st time on 4th yr.
Earth satisfied: a land flowing with milk & honey. Hope N. Messiah-Yeshua